"Please do not bury me.
I will awake from my sleep
at my chosen moment . . ."

So in Wing Tek Lum's chosen moment—the Nanjing Massacre—both literature and history are dangerously awakened. Epigrammatic, elegiac, and luminous, these poems beckon the buried voices of daughters and sons, husbands and wives, soldiers and survivors—Chinese and Japanese alike. This masterful and courageous collection allows us to breathe deeply over the shallows of history and to understand, through poetry, how "the truth shall set us free."

Russell C. Leong, Contributing Editor, *Amerasia Journal*

Wing Tek Lum observes the Nanjing Massacre, stares directly at the slaughtered remains, the historical evidence, and you may well ask why. As tribute to Iris Chang, whose own tortured experience and suicide gives pause: yes. To prod a litany of human disasters, Shoah, Congo, Sabra/ Shatila, My Lai, Cambodia, Darfur, Bosnia, Rwanda, Jenin, Homs: no problem. But I think it's more for company, to join the other messengers in God's waiting room, awaiting reprieve. Have a seat.

Jeffery Paul Chan, author of *Eat Everything Before You Die*

Wing Tek Lum's poems are deeply moving and extremely imaginative. Bridging literature and history, they offer one solution to the almost impossible task of recovering lost voice and experience where no historical records exist.

Daqing Yang, Associate Professor of History and International Affairs, George Washington University

THE NANJING MASSACRE: POEMS

Wing Tek Lum

Bamboo Ridge Press

ISBN 978-0-910043-88-5

This is issue #102 (Fall 2012) of *Bamboo Ridge, Journal of Hawai'i Literature and Arts* (ISSN 0733-0308).

Published by Bamboo Ridge Press

Printed in the United States of America

Indexed in the *Humanities International Complete*

Bamboo Ridge Press is a member of the Council of Literary Magazines and Presses (CLMP).

Typesetting and design: Rowen Tabusa

Cover art: "Nanjing Lotus" (detail from a two-panel painting), 2012, by Noe Tanigawa, encaustic, varnish on canvas, 12" X 54" (per panel)

Interior art: 2009, by Noe Tanigawa, charcoal on vellum, 8.5" X 7.25"
Page 17: "All These Bodies"
Page 55: "At the Foot of Mufu Mountain"
Page 91: "The Professional Mourners"
Page 141: "Where We Left Our Family"
Page 191: "The Beheader"
Page 217: "The Resistance"

Author's photo by Rowen Tabusa

Bamboo Ridge Press is a nonprofit, tax-exempt corporation formed in 1978 to foster the appreciation, understanding, and creation of literary, visual, or performing arts by, for, or about Hawai'i's people. This publication was made possible with support from the Cooke Foundation.

Bamboo Ridge is published twice a year. For subscription information, back issues, or a catalog, please contact:

Bamboo Ridge Press; P.O. Box 61781; Honolulu, HI 96839-1781

(808) 626-1481; brinfo@bambooridge.com
www.bambooridge.com

5 4 3 2 1   12 13 14 15 16

TABLE OF CONTENTS

for Louise Lee Lum

WHAT I LEARNED FROM YOUR COLLEGE ANNUAL

You were considered "The social star of 1929."
You wore wispy bangs unlike most of your classmates,
but also you combed back your short hair
to expose your ears.
When it was cold in Shanghai
it seems that women students wore padded cheongsam
making all of you look like woolen dumplings.
Everyone also wore long white leggings
and shoes with straps across the insteps
which I am told are called Mary Janes.
You joined the church choir and sang alto.
You went by the English spelling of "Li" for your surname
—and not "Lee" which was on your paperwork
when you arrived in Honolulu.
Like you, a large number of students
were actually Cantonese, or from Guangxi.
You played basketball
in a uniform with a sailor's top and black tights.
You were also secretary of the softball team
and served as sports editor
for the school's English bi-weekly.
I discovered your second cousin, slightly older,
was part of the music faculty;
she later lived in Los Angeles but also died young.
In most of your photographs
you smiled close-lipped
except for one where a grin escaped your mouth.
You were not named the prettiest,
and there were others
who published the yearbook poems
in English and Chinese.
You graduated with a Social Science degree

and were active in the YWCA.
In Hong Kong twenty-five years ago
I once met an old couple
who were classmates of yours.
They said there was another classmate
who was sweet on you.
I forgot his name,
and when I looked for the couple in this annual
I could not find them as well.
When you posed, you often tilted your head forward:
my daughter now has this trait.
All of the people in this book
no doubt are now dead
—though the hard truth is,
it was not because they lived out their allotted days.
Unlike you, they stayed,
and their world died so soon after,
before they would reach their primes.

PART ONE

"Heaven has collapsed…"

THE WALL

The first emperor established his capital
in the country's heartland
along the banks of the long river.
His engineers followed the contours
of the site's natural defenses.
The wide, rushing river flanked it on the west.
The mountain shrouded in purple mist,
thick with evergreens,
blocked any approach from the east.
In the north there was a barrier of small lakes
which also provided their drinking water.
Even to the south a tributary served as a moat
wending its way to the river.

The wall itself was raised
upon granite or limestone foundations.
It actually consisted of two walls,
an inner and outer one,
made from bricks fired from special kilns
with brickmakers' names stamped on their sides.
For mortar they mixed lime, tung oil,
and cooked glutinous rice.
After every few layers of brick were laid
they packed the space between the walls
with broken bricks, gravel and yellow earth,
soaking the fill lightly with water,
then tamping it firmly to squeeze out air.
Stone sluices were added to channel rainwater.

The wall was built as high as ten men
standing one atop the other.
Its parapet walk was thick enough

to fit fifteen marching shoulder to shoulder.
It took two hundred thousand laborers
toiling twenty-one years to complete.
Massive and imposing, it was to be
as impregnable as the dynasty,
constructed to last ten thousand years.
Even today much of the wall still stands,
though the city is now known as *Nanjing*,
or the southern capital.
In his day the emperor had named it
Yingtianfu—responding to heaven.

PREFERENTIAL CERTIFICATE

(We absolutely will not kill
anyone who surrenders.)

Any soldier of the Chinese army
not interested in the war of resistance
and who holds up a white flag
or raises both hands
carrying this certificate
may come forward to surrender
and pay allegiance to the Japanese army.
This the Japanese army will affirm,
and will provide full provisions
and offer suitable jobs
as expressions of our preferential treatment.
Intelligent soldiers, why not come?

The Japanese Military Command

THE SEAMSTRESS

"It is nobody's room now."
—Vasily Grossman, *A Writer at War*,
on a young refugee leaving her home

Yes, she has packed all her hard cash,
her ring and brooch,
an extra set of clothes and shoes,
her small tin box of needles and shears,
a cushion of pins
and her measuring tape,
a small bundle of steamed buns,
and a sharp knife,
all wrapped up in a heavy blanket
which she can carry in her arms.
But she has left her mirror and brush,
her scarves and fan,
the embroidered coverlet,
her beloved sewing machine
with its smooth-stepping treadle,
the bolts of cloth she has hoarded,
her larder of rice and coal,
dough figurines from her childhood,
a ceramic pillow
once used by her grandfather,
the now faded paper cuts on the wall.
Whether all of this world will be here
if she ever comes back
does not cross her mind.
She turns to walk away
the moment she shuts the door,
steeling herself
for the days and years to come,

without memories, without tears.
There is only the gunmetal sky overhead,
the white-capped river relentlessly flowing,
mountains rising to razor sharp peaks,
a path often vanishing,
wending through gnarled forests,
the vast, forsaken fields.

OUR SCORCHED EARTH POLICY

We hardboil all our eggs
to carry and eat with ease.

As for the chickens,
they are too numerous.

But we are loathe
to leave them behind

for the invaders to consume
and then thus fortified

come hard on our heels.
So we slaughter them

and stuff ourselves full.
This night is like a grand feast

for a wedding
or one of our festival days.

Though for me
I can taste only my fears.

THE HAND CART

They have loaded the cart
with as much as they can carry,
their one table, a scatter of chairs,
a cast iron kettle, pots and bowls,
dried vegetables and salt fish
wrapped in oil paper,
and bags of rice hidden underneath
inside buckets covered with tarp.
Extra clothing is stuffed into crevices,
a rolled up rug sticks out.
Woven baskets hang from the legs of a ladder.
Everywhere ropes snake under and about
lashing together all that is loose.
Three children sit atop bundles of firewood
weighing down the back as ballast.
The mother, brows knitted,
is perched crosslegged on the table above,
as if in the crow's nest of a boat,
a captain surveying their road ahead.
Her one hand grasps the table's edge
to keep herself from sliding off,
the other clutches their newborn
swaddled in a thick down blanket.
From behind, the father leans into the cart
pushing it forward on its two hard wheels;
it is a balancing act
to keep up the momentum
without scraping the ground
in the front or back.
He must keep them moving
for as long as his legs hold out,
for as far away as they can get.

FLEEING

"I had only one idea…not to
be taken like a rat in Occupied
Paris."
—Simone de Beauvoir,
diary entry for June 9, 1940

A father pushes a hand cart
with possessions stacked so high
he cannot see where he is going.
A wagon drawn by a pony
transports a family
of three generations.
It is so crowded
that no one can sit down.
A grandmother
with golden lotus feet
lies in a wheelbarrow grimacing.
Barges are commandeered
to ferry trunks of antiques
and their curators upstream.
An automobile speeds out the gate
only to be found miles ahead
lying in a ditch, out of petrol.
The early risers
jostle their way onto a train
that never leaves the station.
A lorry is filled with deserters
their guns and ammunition
left in the barracks.
Sniveling children
are propped onto bicycles,
their parents

walking at their sides.
All around them
are others who know only
that they must now flee;
on foot, they move south,
they move west, traveling light,
carrying only hope.

≈

On the side of the road
a western style clock
stands upright
still telling time.
Farther down,
there are abandoned valises,
canvas dufflebags,
a wedding chest
inlaid with mother-of-pearl
and filled with silk,
ceramic cooking pots
swaddled in blankets,
a matching tea set
cradled in its own basket,
photograph albums,
bundles of old aerogrammes
tightly bound with string,
a rattan cage with porcelain cups
for water and seed,
its door now open,
its bird also in flight.

≈

A large family argues under a tree.
The elders cannot continue on.
For half a day
they have been carried
on the backs of their grandsons.
But they are concerned
they are slowing down
everyone else.
They want to stay and rest
and tell the others
to go on ahead;
they will catch up later.
The youngsters also want to leave
but know they never will.

∽

Steamed buns, scallion pancakes,
sticky rice in lotus leaves,
small sacks of millet,
beans and preserved plums,
salt fish, pickled cabbage,
dried scallops and baby shrimp,
bamboo shoots, pumpkin seeds,
black mushrooms and wood fungus,
ginger root, almonds, pine nuts,
one thousand year old eggs,
a tin of sliced pineapple
and a tin of condensed milk
—these days worth
more than their weight
in jade or ivory or gold.

∽

At night, we can hear
explosions in the distance,
the drone of airplanes
passing overhead.
At night, babies cry from hunger,
a woman sobs uncontrollably
fearing she will never
be able to go back.
At night, when lightning strikes,
there is no shelter;
the entire countryside erupts
in one loud thunderclap
that stuns us into silence.

～

The days turn
into marches of endurance
not of speed.
Under darkness
the cold contends with sleep.
Even in our dreams
we trudge along the road,
no matter where it will lead.
We only stop
when a farmer up ahead
approaches with his family
to ask how many more miles
it would take to reach
the city of refuge they seek.

AFTER THE BOMB

A father, face caked with blood,
stumbles aimlessly through the brick rubble,
cradling his lifeless child.
A grandmother drags about
a large bundle; she is searching
for the dead, for their clothing especially,
to keep her family warm at night.
Splinters of glass have peppered
a man's back; he writhes
in pain, face down,
unable to remove them.
An aunt and her niece carry a cleaver
wherever they go; it is to fend off
any looters who come onto the place
where their home once stood.
Police discover a soldier
hidden in an outdoor cistern
used to collect rainwater; his body
is bloated, with splotches of colors,
as if cooked to death.
A young boy walks to the river,
bucket in hand, to carry back water
for his family; he is told
to be on the lookout for any broken furniture
to drag back for their fire.
In a makeshift cellar
three sisters lie together—the firestorm
has consumed them; they are identified
only by the strips of clothing
stuck to their blackened corpses.
The young mother unearths a full jar
of salted vegetables; without hesitation

she decides to tell no one,
not even her husband.
Two girls erect a lean-to
against the last standing wall.
One has burnt arms, but helps, grimacing,
by using her teeth and feet.
Seething, a teenager
methodically works through the remains
of each house in the neighborhood,
seeking her family, but raging
all the while, fists against the sky,
against all the demons
and this cursed bomb that went astray.

THE PEACH BOYS

We were sent by Heaven
to serve the Emperor.
Raised by our devoted parents
as peach boys
now strong and obedient
we sailed across the sea
to this foreign land
to fight the wicked ogres
who raid our islands
who plunder and rape
who enslave small children
and torch our homes.

We can see them strutting
high above, along their parapets
bald men with protruding horns
bellowing taunts
mouths reeking of human blood
lungs full of opium
the women hobbling
on dainty feet
wombs twisted, shriveled dry
their long fingernails
glistening in the sunlight
daggers pointing us to hell.

Our airplanes attack
like the pheasant
swooping down from the skies

stabbing away
with its talons and beak.
Our cannons pummel their gates
like the monkey
its long arms whirling furiously.
Our tanks steamroll inexorably
through their streets
like the dog ready to pounce
its powerful bite an instant death.

We tighten our white headbands
and follow our leader
straight into battle
without hesitation.
He is our pink-cheeked hero
stout of heart, unwavering
eyes flashing
all that is noble
all that is good.
We would surely give up
our lives for him
—our beloved Momotaro.

THE NIGHT BEFORE

Our commander assembled our company.
He told us that at dawn
we would lead the charge
to breach the wall. We were to carry
as much ammunition as possible
but only one day's rations.
The next night the food inside the city
would be ours for the taking.
We would without question be victorious.
We would fight bravely,
we would fight fiercely,
but some of us would fall.
We clipped our hair and fingernails
to send back to our families
if our bodies were not recovered.
We spoke of home. Some of us
wrote letters, fingered temple beads
and tucked away our good luck charms.
We cleaned our rifles once again.
We sang songs about cherry blossoms
falling from the branch, petals
scattered in the wind,
their fragrance lingering on forever.
Voices wavered, with lumps in our throats,
eyes misty. But we cheered together.
We shared sake, toasting our company,
our commander, our emperor and country.
The last of us threw down our cups,
porcelain shattering on the ground.

RUNNING

Our captain cajoles us to stay and fight.
We have to protect this capital,
the civilians caught inside, our nation at stake.
Our defenses are only as strong
as the weakest link. No surrender,
no retreats. Here we must stand our ground.

But I sense the sergeants sneaking away.
Shells are battering the old city walls,
dive bombers blowing up buildings with ease,
all around us machine guns ricocheting death.
Soon bridges will collapse,
our gates entered. There will be no escape.

We throw away our rifles, throw off our uniforms.
I trade my boots for a tailor's old rags.
I am still worried—
with our shorn hair, the calluses on our hands,
we may still be marked men.

Some of us head for the river
to find a boat, to swim if possible,
to hide shivering under the piers.
I race down the boulevards
carried forward by crowds,
mothers with toddlers hanging on their backs,
old men pushing carts,
other soldiers yelling to make way,
everyone with a bundle,
and all about us fires burning.

Sometimes the throng lifts me up,
sometimes my feet trample upon bodies,

derelict, sticky and wet.
Shoulder to shoulder, I cannot look down.
I cannot see above the swell of heads.
Where I am, I have no idea.
All I wish for is to find a crack in the ground,
a hole in a wall to slip on through.

A grenade lands nearby, and our mob scatters.
A tank lumbering down the lane
herds us back together.
I hide in a side alley to catch my breath;
smoke fills my lungs, sears my eyes.
All I can hear is the crackling of guns,
houses crumbling, the pleas of women.

Dazed, I pick my way through the rubble
heading upwards outside the walls
through a small clutch of woods.
There is a graveyard on the side of the hill,
a stubble of tombstones.
I crawl up to one
as much for the shelter among the dead
as to provide me warmth.
I pray even my pursuers must need sleep.

But explosions still stun the night.
Below I see a great inferno being wrought,
the acrid scent rising up
of executions, plunder and rape.
I do not want to be part of this misery any more.
I pull myself up, I keep on running.

I HOLD MY BREATH

We hit them hard. So many are cut down
by our initial charge. The few left standing

flee and we give chase, full throttle
through the field of newly dead and wounded.

There is no time to go around.
I keep driving straight, noting every soft impact.

Our tank sways gently, losing traction
upon this uncertain ground, a small boat

plowing through the waves. I hold
my breath; in my heart I pray for mercy.

HAIKU

AFTER THE FIREFIGHT

surrounding snow keeps melting
our light machine gun
has not yet cooled down

≈

ON THE ROAD

a body flat on the road
crushed by passing tanks
face in bas relief

≈

BLOOD

splattered on my shirt
this blood must be another's
—I am still alive

≈

TAKING OFF MY BOOTS

I dry off my swollen feet
—overgrown toenails
now need to be pared

≈

COOKING RICE

we use their helmets
but mine keeps leaking water
—a clean bullet hole!

STRETCHER BEARERS

We had made it halfway down the hill
before we noticed
that the buddy we were lugging
was no longer breathing.
We still wanted to bring his body back
so he could return home.
But many more up there
had been hit.
We decided to roll him off
by a shattered tree
and make our way to the summit
to find another of our wounded.
It hurt—but then again
maybe it did not matter
to this guy anymore.
He had crossed over to another world.
It was for us
to help others persevere in ours.

HEAVEN HAS COLLAPSED

"I hallucinated a couple of times."
—Bernard Coon, in Patrick O'Donnell,
Into the Rising Sun

I wake up in a field of corpses.
All around me are the dead, as I have been
—for hours or days, I do not know.
But now I am alive again.
The raw odor of rotting flesh scours my nostrils.
The incessant buzz of flies swarms in my ears.
Plump maggots, tingling of death,
fester within my wounds.

But I cannot get up; I struggle to move.
Soon the demons will arrive with their dogs
to seek out those they have not yet slain,
to strip us of our weapons and valuables,
to interrogate and torture us,
to use us as their diversions.

With all my might I crawl about,
my shattered squad now cast away,
making my way through their bodies,
or parts of bodies
—a face ripped open by shrapnel,
a mangled arm, a severed foot in its boot,
blood, a thin cracked layer,
everywhere staining the ground.

Heaven has collapsed;
the air is thick with broken souls,
with nowhere to go.
This is the cruelest maze.

My only thought is to follow the setting sun,
hoping it will lead to where we came from.
It takes me the whole night to reach our lines.

Our doctor later congratulates me on my luck
—the maggots have eaten away the gangrene—
as he pours in the alcohol to kill them.

IN A DESERTED CAMP

We are so hungry
that when we come across
a hidden crate of canned meat
we lose all discipline
and climb over each other
to grab what we can.
We do not notice
the airplane overhead
until it starts strafing us.
Everyone dives for cover.
And when my buddy gets hit
instead of attending
to his wounds
I just scramble for his tins.

MY BUDDY

The two of us
were in a foxhole

and a grenade
was lobbed inside.

We were taught
to act quickly:

you get out
or you get it out.

My buddy scrambled
over the edge.

I scooped it up
and flung it away.

But it went
in his direction,

and exploded
blowing off his hand.

This was luck
—but whose?

He was sent home.
I fight on.

INSIDE ZHONGSHAN GATE

We created an altar
for those who had died.
Then we drank and we sang
to our everlasting victory.

I boasted that we would conquer
this whole country in six months' time
But our sergeant did not laugh,
he did not argue.

It will take us years,
if not forever, was all he replied.
I did not believe him,
chiding such gloom.

So we bet on a dish
of the freshest yellowtail
to be paid up
when our platoon went home.

I lost the wager,
and ended the war as a POW.
He lost his life at this gate
when his body was blown to smithereens.

A REAL SOLDIER

After the skirmish they retreated.
We had a chance to rest up.
My buddy went behind a tree
to take a dump.
But he quickly returned
and motioned me over.
I saw this body lying on its side.
We knew by the uniform
that he was one of them.
At first I thought the guy was dead.
But my buddy pointed out
that even though he was not moving
the eyes blinked
and we could see him breathing.
He must have been wounded
or paralyzed somehow.
He was looking at us
but could not do anything about it.
We gave him a few pokes
and checked the hands
to make sure there were no weapons.
He made no noise.
I wondered if he was in pain
or maybe in no pain at all.
My buddy could not wait
and pulled down his pants.
He squatted beside the guy
and took his crap.
The turd landed
right in front of his face.
My buddy laughed
that this guy would now be stuck

with the sight and the smell
of a real soldier.
I thought this was disgusting
and said so.
But my buddy shot back
that I had better watch out.
If their side caught me
in the same situation
they would not hesitate
to crap into my nose and mouth
just to see me gasp my last breath.

THE NEAR DEAD

They lie cast about
as if by a sudden whirlwind,
some faces pressed into the ground,
some staring up at the sky,
some without faces anymore.
There are bodies
that are contorted, arched
or curled up and inert
like a pond snail pried from its shell,
some with arms or legs splayed
or with arms or legs
broken, blown off, crushed.
Blood pools from under the bodies,
bubbles up, oozes into rust,
is splattered on their uniforms,
their life breaths hushed, swirling,
hovering above, sucked within,
butterflies too stunned to fly home.
Our sergeant, a compassionate man,
picks his way through the corpses
clutching a torch and his beads,
pointing to this one or that,
the few still writhing
or uttering a slow moan,
the glint of an eye now raw and weary,
a rabbit of dread,
and we follow, bayonets poised
then thrusting quickly,
aiming true, into their hearts,
rending souls,
these still wavering,
these rice birds darting in and out.

I AM NOT DEAD

"I've written several times in this diary about
the body of the Chinese soldier…still lying
unburied near my house…I have stopped trying
to get the poor devil buried, but I hereby record
that he, though very dead, still lies above
ground."

—John Rabe, diary entry for January 22, 1938

I am not dead.
I wait on my back on this street
surrounded by the rubble of buildings,
discarded weapons, and charred corpses
as the tanks rumble by
as marauding soldiers scurry about
as the refugees of the city flee or hide.
The bayonet wound in my left calf has bled me white.
The two bullets which shattered my chest
now lodge in my liver
weighting me to the ground.
The brittle cold has seared my lungs,
my ears, my gaping mouth.
So I lie here hibernating,
day and night, maggots under my skin,
stiff, desiccated, flaking away, layer by layer.

Please do not bury me.
I will awake from my sleep
at my chosen moment
when the night is ripe
when even dreams are tucked away.
The sky will be overcast, no moon will shine through.
My body will rise up
arms heavy as anvils, swirling like scythes

my shout like ten thousand demons
my eyes blazing straight into the hearts of our enemies
to strike them down
sever their heads and slit their bellies
grind up their souls into so many pieces of dust
to be scattered across this land
—a land to which no sun will ever return.

ALL THESE BODIES

on the ground
soldiers who were ready
to defend us
but now lie broken
cast aside
all slain
all decomposing
flesh to mud
wounds open
bared
maggots festering
rats all in a feast—

what comes to mind
in this moment
of despair
is the old sage
on his deathbed:

forget the coffin
he told his disciples
leave me
with no jade
or jewels
instead of the worms
and ants
to eat me
why not the crows?

A RIVER'S LAMENT

Ravenous birds stalk my banks,
their sleek, rapier-sharp beaks pecking away
at only the most succulent flesh.

Wide-eyed fish swarm my surface
darting through the rich clouds of blood
engorging themselves into a stupor.

Baby eels snuggle within the skeletons,
bone jungles scattered about my mud bottom,
some broken, crushed, some bleach white.

Hulking turtles toy with clumps of hair,
a surfeit of tangled strands floating by,
pulled by my current to the open sea.

A KIMONO

Its field consists of horizontal bands,
alternating a rich victory blue
and a mottled beige suggestive of the earth.
Overlaid are four roundels
—one depicting an airplane seen from underneath
with broad, outstretched wings, propellers spinning,
another of a tank, its front hull proud,
as if sticking out its chest,
its treads advancing large and resolute.
In a third picture, three round-faced boys
wear helmets, khaki uniforms and knapsacks.
Two of them stand poised, their right feet forward,
rifles pointed, ready to lunge bayonets.
The third child, mouth open, rallies the others,
his right hand waving a sword above his head,
while his left holds fast to their military flag,
a red rising sun with rays.
Following them is their white and brown puppy,
equally plump, with large eyes,
its snub tail up, watchful, protecting their rear.
There is one last circle,
a cityscape row of masonry buildings
with a balloon flying from atop one,
carrying aloft in a long trailing banner
the words *Nanjing Occupied* in red.

This is how we can tell when this kimono was made.
From its small size we know it was for a toddler,
probably for a young son to be worn just once
for his ceremonial visit to the temple
—perhaps for Boys' Day,
or his third or fifth birthday—

but with a modern print on traditional dress.
The family likely wanted to join in the celebration,
to commemorate this first blush of victory in 1937.
Back then it did not matter that in faraway China
homes were reduced to rubble by those sleek bombers,
that fleeing crowds were run over by tanks,
that surrendering soldiers were tied to poles
and used for bayonet practice.
This was a small price for such glory,
though by the end it became much too expensive
as to beggar belief, engendering outright denial.
By the end, all that was left was this kimono,
this vestige from when the war was young and grand.

PART TWO

"...his new life of death."

AT THE FOOT OF MUFU MOUNTAIN

We tell them that they are going to an island
in the middle of the Yangtze.
They wait together, hands bound, each of them,
on the bank of the river
surrounded by our semicircle of machine guns.
I am on the far right.

We are standing on a flood plain
at the foot of Mufu Mountain
outside the walls of the captured capital.
We wait about for the whole afternoon.
In the channel there are two small boats
to ferry them across,
but then they disappear.
It is now growing dark.
We mill about. Rumors fly.

The order to fire is given.
We use heavy machine guns and light machine guns.
I fire my rifle at individuals in the crowd
aiming at those not yet hit.
I shoot, and continue to shoot.
Prisoners keep dropping
crying out above the din of our guns
in pain, in fury, in anguish;
the air revolts into a single great roar.

They fall in clumps onto the ground;
others fall on top of them.
Some try to escape and climb on top of these bodies,
even with their hands tied behind their backs.
How futile it is. More scramble
on top these others. The bodies pile up—

a human pillar ten feet tall.
Then it collapses.
And then again bodies pile up on bodies.
We keep shooting.
And then another pillar forms,
and then collapses.
And a third time. We keep shooting.

It is very dark now, the moon covered by clouds.
A misty rain is falling,
and wind from the north stings my ears.
We spend the rest of the night
bayoneting each corpse,
one by one, until dawn. Not many are still alive.
I can pull out my bayonet easily
except when I stab someone in the head,
when it makes a clicking sound.

We pour gasoline on some of the bodies
and set them on fire.
Winter clothing ignites quickly.
Anyone still moving is stabbed again.
We wade through the muck of the dead,
our boots and leggings growing sticky,
their blood, their spilled out guts,
their flesh ripped apart, splattered all about.

We shove the corpses into the river.
It takes us the rest of the night.
My arms grow sore; I cannot lift them.
Other troops arrive to relieve us.
Returning to camp, before I fall asleep,
I write in my diary:
We are victorious.
Today we have killed 13,500 prisoners.

THE RED CIRCLE

With a nub of red chalk
our sergeant marks off
a crude circle in the center
of the chest. Then he tells
these new guys
that this is the one area
they are prohibited
from stabbing.
That is where the heart is,
he says. They are
learning how to use a bayonet.
But today we can round up
only five prisoners
for our platoon. We have
to keep them alive
for as long as we can.

NEW RECRUITS

He jabs me with the tip of his blade.
Then he steps back
holding his rifle waist high.
He takes several deep breaths.
He hardly looks at me,
but suddenly lunges.
I am lucky I can wriggle about
even though my hands are bound
to a pole behind my back.
He has stood too far away
so I can quickly twist myself around
and catch his bayonet
in my side, under my rib cage.
It still hurts, I grimace,
the pain howls through my body.
My shirt is soaked with blood.
I now understand what is happening.
This is for real, I am to die.
I try to resist, but I feel faint.
I groan, my knees give way,
and I slide down the pole.
Other soldiers start yelling.
They point to my chest, my belly.
He was supposed to kill me
but has not.
So he tries again
this time standing above me,
his eyes fixed,
staring straight into my heart.
I am immobile, in a squat,
my head leaning forward towards him.
I growl, I scream,

I beg for mercy.
This time he stabs me
once, then again, and again,
cracking my ribs,
tearing apart my guts,
slashing my throat, my face.
I die, but he continues
his thrusts and grunts
until he is covered
with the splatterings of my flesh
mingled with his sweat,
his frenzied tears
inside my lungs,
the death of my life
now woven into
his new life of death.

THROWN INTO THE EARTH

as if into the sea
but there is no buoyancy
for the body to rise
to the surface
no room for legs to kick
or arms to paddle

submerged underground
there is no light
no sound

the little air
within the shoveled-over dirt
is sucked up
in no time

gasping for more
small clumps of soil
fall into the mouth
and nostrils and eyes

panic seizes
the struggle to breathe
becomes all consuming

the heart keeps pounding
lungs collapse

muscles go slack
the brain in shock

the soul
            no escape

THE BEHEADER

The sword carried my mother's spirit.
I bathed it with water
poured gently from a small dipper.
Then I checked my stance
using the back of the blade
to touch his neck ever so lightly
to gauge my reach.
I turned the blade over,
lifted it above my right shoulder,
and swung hard.

There was a soft, swishing noise.
The blade sliced clean
through the flesh and bone.
The head dropped off in front of him,
a thud on the ground, face down.
The neck seemed to contract slightly,
then two streams of blood spurted forth,
and his body slumped forward.
Then the blood stopped.

I was nervous
because my blade had been bent.
I checked its rivet; it had held.
I did not enjoy this duty
unlike some of the other officers
who uttered a cry, as if cheering,
at each beheading.
I did not toy with the prisoners either,
first loudly going through the motions
to deceive them into thinking
that they had already been cut
and then when they raised their heads

like some stupid deer
striking them for real.

Some of them swayed;
they had been tortured, half starved.
Maybe they were praying
or hoping that it was just a test.
They just kept their heads lowered.
We did not blindfold them
—but what they saw at those last moments
I do not know.

I struck again and again,
each man kneeling along the line.
I became flustered, out of breath, perspiring.
Wiping my forehead, I also wiped my tears.
A few heads I lopped off neatly.
For the others,
my blade got caught in the bone,
the head clinging somehow
to the front flap of the neck,
flopping under the chest
as the torso fell.

Occasionally I had to stop
to wash off the blood turned sticky,
the bits of flesh.
My blade was still bent,
and I had to straighten it with my hands.
The rivet also started to loosen,
creating a rattle.
I hastened to complete my job.
The whole village was wailing.
Thick blood spewed all over.
I was angry and confused.
I was determined to honor my mother.

A PERVERSION

"hakuheisen"—an official term meaning *"to
fight with a drawn sword"*
—Gordon L. Rottman, *FUBAR*

Yammering all the time.
He should wear a beret and wave a megaphone
since he acts so much like a movie director
telling us where to dig a pit
and then that we have to stand around it waiting.
He also orders the photographers around,
some kneeling here, others standing there,
a battery of cameras ready to shoot photos
within a split second of each other.
When he thinks the stage is set
our captain waves in one of the prisoners
pointing to the place
where he must get down on all fours,
a spot facing the pit near the edge,
and then how he should sit back on his haunches,
his upper torso leaning slightly forward,
his head raised just so.
This fanatic gesticulates, cajoles,
squats, and squints his eyes,
double checking the angle of the captive's neck,
and that the collar is not in the way.
Then he announces that everything is ready.
And we all have to watch him, solemnly,
remove his sword and wipe it down,
as if it were his prick.
He stands on the far side
holding his sword with one hand raised high,
giving warning to the photographers to get ready.

Then with one big swoop
he cuts off the prisoner's head.
It drops into the pit, and the body slumps over.
Our captain utters a victory shout.
We have seen this sight too often.
At first we were shocked and fascinated,
but now there is only disgust.
This pompous fool—all he wants
is for one of the cameras
to capture the very moment
when his blade has sliced clean through,
the head still hanging in mid-air
as if in flight from the neck,
which is already slumping
from its body's weight,
revealing the desired slightest of gaps.
These poor saps just a week ago
were enemies who shot at us;
but it was their generals who snuck away
leaving them to surrender.
So now they are starving and without weapons.
How courageous is that—
to fight with a drawn sword
when your opponent has none?
This is a perversion of the warrior spirit,
and we will be the ones
who will lose our heads for it.

MY REWARD

The stealing, the women—
I enjoyed them. But when we were
out on break, wandering through
a neighborhood, burnt out
or half bombed to rubble,
I'd look for bodies, whether
they were charred
or full of maggots, or just
lying there still, on the floor
of an outdoor cooking area,
or slumped over
in their store, or
in a narrow alleyway, some
with their mouths
agape, or others their jaws
frozen shut, unable
to be pried open.
My interest was the
gold. So many of these
city folk had
fillings or even whole teeth
clad in the metal.
I could not
miss an opportunity: it was
like a drug for me. As my buddies
ransacked a deserted home
for money or food or
antiques, I looked
for the dead and, finding
a corpse, could not help but
open up its mouth to check
for gold. I never got used to

the stench, the rot
being freed up from inside
the gut, so overpowering,
as I worked the jaw. But if
I spied any glint of metal, nothing
stopped me from
taking out my two pliers,
holding down the rest
of the teeth with
one while I pulled out
the tooth with the other. Back
in our barracks
I washed my hands and face
clean, and made sure to stick
the pliers and tooth
in a pot of boiling water
to kill any
germs. Then with my bayonet
I carefully picked
out the filling, making sure
to scrape off as much as I could
onto my white handkerchief. Sometimes
I dreamed I could
make a fire hot enough to
melt out whatever flecks were still
left inside the cavity.
But after a while I knew
it was not worth the effort any
more and threw away
the tooth. The gold would be added to
the rest of my collection.
At night, I kneaded this hoard
with my pliers and

the butt of my canteen, over
and over again, a secret
pleasure, until it became a malleable
lump, a ritual recalling when we used
to pound sticky rice
on New Year's Day. I hid
the growing yellow ball wrapped in
the handkerchief in my left
pants pocket. I could live with
the bullets and
explosions. The gold was my reward.

THE BOOTS

We pulled the bodies
out of the rubble.
My eyes immediately spied
the shiny ankle boots
on one of the corpses,
most likely a new officer.
The soles of my shoes
had worn through.
I wanted his and wondered out loud
how warm they would be,
so thick and smooth.
But he had died some time ago,
his body frozen stiff.
Again and again
I tried to pull the boots off,
but they clung to the feet
like bark on a tree.
Everyone laughed,
and someone even suggested
I cut through the leather
and then try to sew it back up.
But I came up with another idea,
and with my bayonet
I stabbed away around the knees
chipping off flesh,
hard as wood.
Finally I hit bone all around
and sought to pry open the joints.
I stacked a mound of bricks
underneath the knees
like a fulcrum,
and then with some others

weighing down on the chest
I jumped on top of his feet
to crack the legs off.
Once they were severed,
I cradled them in my arms
like two logs
over to where the cooks
had built a fire.
By the end of our meal
the feet had thawed
soft enough for me
to tug off the boots.
I sat on the ground
holding the exposed knee joint
while my buddy clutched the heel.
I scooped out
the rest of the flesh,
and cleaned the insides
flushing them thoroughly
with hot water.
Quickly I dried them
inside and out.
I polished the leather
before trying them on.
The boots were a size too large,
but I just needed to steal
a second pair of socks to wear.
Now they will last me
throughout the war
and keep me warm and dry.
It is my luck—
I surely will survive.

PRAGMATIC

Ammunition and supplies need to be carried.
Men from the village are press ganged. When a few drop
from exhaustion, they are killed, and others
are quickly found to take their places. Farmers are forced
to wade through a manure pit to retrieve hidden valuables;
though nothing is found, half of them freeze to death.
When army rations taste bland, a family's cellar
is plundered. A small town needs to be cowed, so the elders
are beheaded in a square, the townspeople beseeching.
A resistance fighter is caught; information must be tortured
out of him. Too many prisoners of war have surrendered
like cowardly dogs. There is no place to keep or feed them,
so they are slaughtered en masse. New draftees need
to practice bayonet charges, so prisoners are tied to stakes
and stabbed repeatedly. When a machine gun needs
to be tested, other prisoners are rounded up as targets.
Factory workers are sent across a field that must be cleared
of mines. When a teacher fails to bow, an officer
as an example pummels him senseless. The watchdogs
are hungry, and a man is bound to a tree, his flesh
sliced off, strip by strip, to feed them. Young soldiers
roaming the city need diversions: they raid homes
for women to rape. A brother tries to protect
his elder sister; he is summarily shot. Those women
who protest or resist are killed as bothersome;
the others who succumb are also killed to prevent them
from speaking up. Some women that are kidnapped are kept
in a hospital to wash clothes by day; throughout the night
they are also raped. Houses are looted indiscriminately
—money, food, jewelry, clothing, furniture—to be consumed,
or worn, or sent back home. To hide the evidence, the houses
are then put to the torch. When too many corpses

litter the streets, refugees are seized to dig mass graves;
afterwards, they too are pushed in and buried alive.
Other bodies are disposed of, piled up into mounds,
doused with gasoline, and set on fire. Or they are shoved
into the river, or just left to rot amidst the rest
of the rubble. Some of the dead are dumped into a canal
which needs to be crossed; boards and doors are then laid
on the top and sides to form a corpse bridge.
A young girl keeps wailing over her mother's dead body
all night; soldiers smother her to get back to sleep.

CAPRICIOUS

A dozen villagers are tied wrist to wrist
in a small circle, and a grenade is tossed in the middle.
A fetus is gouged out of a pregnant woman
to satisfy a bet by soldiers as to whether it is a boy
or girl. Refugees seeking shelter are locked
in a house which is ringed with firewood and set on fire.
Kerosene is poured onto a trio of peasants;
the invaders take potshots to see who can ignite them.
A toddler is dropped into a well on a whim.
Marauding troops force an old man to shelter
and cook for them; the next morning they throw him
into a large kettle and boil him to death. Out of the blue,
a man's throat is slit while he sits in a privy.
Surrendering prisoners of war clutch leaflets
promising leniency but are executed on the spot.
Others who surrender are roped together in columns
and led away to die. Another prisoner is pulled out
of a crowd and ordered to go down on all fours;
a sergeant then sits down on top of his back
to have his hair cut. Another captor receives a watch
as a bribe; suddenly full of pity, he lets two prisoners go
but somehow not the watch donor. Two sub-lieutenants start
a contest to see who can behead one hundred men first.
Heads that have been chopped off line a wall, ear to ear;
another head has a cigarette butt popped into its mouth.
By the side of a road, four bodies sit with their heads
placed on their laps. Soldiers ready to execute a student
unexpectedly hear a woman's voice nearby and give chase;
the student is left on his knees, his pants leg soaked
with urine. Without warning, women are grabbed
off the street, or their homes are broken into, or a group
of schoolgirls is kidnapped to serve in a barracks.

A clearing or park is turned into a makeshift brothel.
Nuns in a temple are raped, so are three generations
in their own home, and out of curiosity, babies too.
A company marches back to their bivouac: interspersed
within the sea of uniforms the pale white flesh
of their captives stands out. Vaginas are stuffed
with all manner of objects, even grenades;
breasts are cut off. Flesh from a woman's thigh is used
as filling for dumplings. A live heart is cut out
as an appetizer to be served with wine. A guard is insulted
seeing a young woman smoking in public; he forces her
to strip naked, her hands bound behind with her belt.
Returning home, she commits suicide. An old woman
with bound feet is forced to stand on a tree stump
for hours; each time she falls off she is propped back up.

THE RESISTANCE

> "According to records, hundreds of
> officers and men [still left after the
> Japanese had occupied Nanjing]…attacked
> the heavily-guarded Ministry of Railways
> …[but eventually] were encircled by
> Japanese troops. The uprising failed,
> but the brave rebels died a hero's death.
> Most remain anonymous…"
>
> —Xu Zhigeng, *Lest We Forget: Nanjing Massacre, 1937*

Two corpses rot in the boulevard;
whatever the dogs have left
is picked over by rats.
A tank crashes through a wall, then veers away.
From where we hide in our basement
we still hear the crackle of machine guns,
though these sounds have given way
to the screams of women in our neighborhood,
day and night, in agony, being raped repeatedly.
The weather has turned cold;
cowards that we are,
most of us have already cast off our uniforms
and now huddle in these peasant clothes
without blankets, without fire.
We dare not go out for food or water.
Only after we smell the smoke
from the house behind us all ablaze
do we escape through the alleyway
to the cul-de-sac where we buried our weapons.
We have three rifles, we have a few grenades.
Airplanes buzz over our quarter.
One of us announces through his clenched teeth:

Better to fight than to be stuck like pigs!
Two crybabies beg to leave and slink away.
The rest of us plan our revenge:
sniper attacks, a slit throat,
Molotov cocktails thrown into an officers' mess.
Who knows what will befall us?
Who knows how long this misery will last?
Every hour feels like the demon's boot
crushing our heads deeper into the ground.
History will record the heroes and victims
—but never fugitives like us.
We are the nameless of the city.
Though it may be pillaged and razed,
though marauders may come and go,
we will remain in the attics, the sewers,
under the rubble that was once homes.
We will be the murmur
in the memories of those who survive,
the smudges on the windowpane,
the blood odor rising in the evening breeze.

THE SNIPER

"The infamous Nanjing Massacre was, in
good part, sparked by Japanese fear of
'plainclothesmen:' Chinese soldiers
who shed their uniforms to act as
snipers or saboteurs."

—Dennis Showalter, "Storm over the Pacific"

With this bullet
my aim is true.
From across the cobblestone square
I bring down an officer.
He is hurled backward
as if hit by a fist of wind
even before he hears my gunshot.
The rest of them
dive for cover,
cry out for help,
shoot wildly about.

With this bullet
their demon hearts roil.
Squads are dispatched
to flush me out.
But I have already snuck away
hiding my rifle
atop the attic beam.
In my stolen clothes
and hair grown out,
no one stops me on the street,
no one sees me.

With this bullet
our ancestors grieve.

The soldiers march out
a dozen shopkeepers
and force them to their knees.
This is their arithmetic
of retribution.
They take their time
to unsheathe their swords.
Taunting,
they know I am watching.

With this bullet
we await death's kiss.
These cityfolk curse me
for continuing their misery.
But I shed no tears for them.
Sooner or later
we will all be murdered.
Better to take revenge
while we can.
I line up my sights
and take a deep breath.

IN THE DARKROOM

"Killing for Fun!"
—the title of an article
in *Look* (November 22, 1938)

They were as small
as the palm of my daughter's hand,
yet even without a magnifying glass
we could see each image so crisp and clear
revealing a horror, like a firecracker,
the slow burn of its fuse
suddenly bursting into shock,
helplessness and rage.

> *A man kneels next to a stream.*
> *An officer stands above him*
> *pushing down his head to expose his neck;*
> *in the foreground another man*
> *also on his knees, slumps over,*
> *his head lying on the ground*
> *in the crook of his arm.*

The invaders pouched their negatives
from the front lines back to our city.
We worked the night shift
to process the film.
Mostly, the pictures were much the same
—some with soldiers atop parapets,
their arms raised in victory,
others depicting a squad, off duty,
relaxing in front of a plaza
or on the steps of a ministry building.

Five others in civilian clothes
are led down into a pit
about to be buried alive;
a crowd of onlookers, in uniform,
rings the edge, surrounding them,
a silent wall.

Yet there were also images
of other events that they wished to capture;
these were the ones that gave us pause.
My co-worker, disgusted,
vowed to destroy the film.
But our owner, one of their countrymen,
wanted to keep up with the demand
and pressed us hard to soon return
every negative and print.
So instead we took
to secretly making extra copies
where we could.

A glum-faced boy is tethered to a pole.
In front, a bespectacled new recruit
holds a rifle, bayonet fixed,
as an officer instructs him
on how to thrust or slash,
on where to aim,
on where to kill.

We passed the prints from friend to friend.
I heard they made their way to another city,
and a few, even months later,
were published in a magazine
outside the country.
This was what we could do to spread the word,
our hope to bring to light

for the world to see
what could not otherwise be described
to be believed—
these indictments of the demons' own making.

A VILLAGE BURIAL

Four bodies lie slumped over
at the pond's edge,
one prone, the others on their sides curled up.
They are wearing soldier's uniforms,
ragged and caked with mud,
shorn of their belts, one without shoes.
They have been decapitated,
the spaces above their necks
where their heads should have been now empty,
the feeling of something missing,
unnerving like a small pin boring through
to prick the heart.
The heads are soon discovered,
floating, half submerged, in shallow waters
—no doubt dumped or kicked in.
They are waterlogged, rapidly decomposing,
one still with spectacles.
Each body is laid out on the bank,
turned over onto its back,
and heads are pressed on top of the necks
to see which fits.
It is hard to determine
which matches are correct
—the long, thin face perhaps
goes with the one with slender fingers,
or maybe another set can be paired
because of the same darker complexion.
They look like they belong, and yet do not.
Together they are loaded onto a two-wheeled cart
and pulled up to the mountains
to a burial pit dug in the hard earth
for all the recent dead.

But it does not seem right
to cast these four so haphazardly
among the other corpses,
though some are also maimed, with severed arms,
their bellies blown out.
So one last attempt is made
to set them down gently,
to rejoin each head to its rightful body.
Hopefully then one of them at least
might be reborn whole,
to re-enter this desecrated world again,
to seek revenge for himself and his comrades,
rending apart these invaders,
hacking limbs, ripping out entrails,
crushing bone, and shredding flesh,
splattering every drop of their blood
across this wide, perverted face of hell.

THE CURSE

One day the sun will rise, and in a flash
the sky will turn brilliant white
as if drained of color,
dazzling blind your sister's eyes.
A shock of intense heat
will sear through your father
instantly consuming him,
his clothes, his hair, muscle and bone.
A roar of wind will swat your mother
into the air, slamming her to the ground,
her limbs crushed and twisted,
a tattered rag doll.
Buildings will collapse,
wooden houses engulfed in flames,
your streets, all rubble and debris.
Charred corpses, maggots festering,
will litter the flattened landscape
and clog your streams.
Survivors will stagger without direction,
deaf and dazed, faces bright red,
skin peeled off, hanging in strips.
A thick haze of stench and dust and ash
will hang over your city like a pall.
There will be only stillness,
and large liquid black drops will fall,
heaven sent, eating away your flesh.
It will be our rain of retribution.

ARMY DOCTORS

If a soldier's arm is lacerated
by shrapnel, we need to know

how to apply a tourniquet,
where to amputate, how to close up

the stump. If he is shot
in the stomach, we must quickly

be able to follow the penetration,
extract the bullet, and sew back

any severed intestines. For a wound
in the throat, because of the blood

accumulating, we will have to cut
into the windpipe, to insert a tube

for breathing. These procedures
we give demonstrations on

for other doctors leaving
for the front. Only for an appendicitis

attack is it difficult to train.
The organ should swell and harden.

But the farmer we work on
has nothing wrong with him, so his

is hard to find. It takes us
several incisions. That is unusual.

UNIT 1644

"Plague was proudly referred to
as *a Nanjing speciality*."
—Simon Winchester, *The River*
at the Center of the World

The lumber was kept in cages
in the Lumber Storage Facility
of the Anti-Epidemic Water Supply Unit,
on the fourth floor of a hospital annex
surrounded by high walls, barbed wire,
electric fences, and patrolling dogs.

White surgical gowns and masks
were worn at all times,
along with rubber boots
and gloves that came up to their shoulders.
No photographs were allowed;
all mail was censored.

Disinfectant mats were laid
in the entryways to the floor
so that shoes could be wiped clean.
Ringing the perimeter walls inside
was a trough of running water
to contain the spread of fleas.

The fleas, some of which were transparent,
were bred in large gasoline cans,
and fed with blood.
Elsewhere, lice and rodents,
even squirrels,
were cultivated in quantities.

The logs were bitten by the fleas or lice
carrying anthrax, typhoid,
cholera, or bubonic plague.
Or they were injected
with venoms from snakes or blowfish,
cyanide, arsenic, or other toxins.

Notes were scrupulously taken
as the logs convulsed, gasped for breath,
threw up, lay paralyzed, or defecated blood.
After autopsy, they were incinerated,
their bones ground down,
their ashes smudging the sky.

DOUBLE CRIMES

They squat, heads bowed,
tethered together, like cowering dogs.
A few look up,
grimacing, or with faces of contempt.
Many are wounded
and groan incessantly.
They look starved
and plead with their eyes.
This platoon of cowards
will slow us down.
It is easier
to line them up and shoot them all
than to let them live
and maybe fight against us again.

The whole squad takes turns.
This woman and this girl
keep wailing and writhing.
Real monkey-like.
Their skins are dark like monkeys too.
Afterwards they lie
with legs splayed
as if to close them
would be too painful.
The older one retches and moans.
The younger one scowls
as if cursing us under her breath.
We stab them once each
in their bellies.
They will not talk.

~

We take the old man's overcoats,
his chickens from the coops in back,
a kettle hanging from a rafter,
the gold rings hidden
in the night soil bucket.
He just stands there,
po-faced, in a corner,
a dumb bug, without moving,
without uttering a word of protest.
He just watches.
Who cares what he is thinking?
We keep him inside,
and set fire to the hut.
We have been told
to get rid of evidence.

PART THREE

"…except always to suffer
our every bidding."

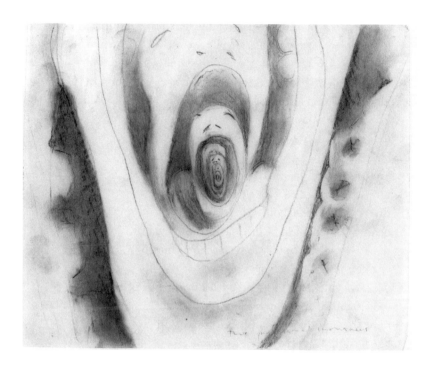

NANJING, DECEMBER, 1937

Thousands tethered like cattle, herded like sheep
into the mountains, the suburbs, the city squares,
into the gullies and waterfront,
to be skewered like pigs, mounted from behind like goats,
castrated, pummeled senseless, clubbed to death,
to be buried alive in ditches dug by themselves,
buried to their waists, their guts ripped out by dogs,
to be run over by tanks, drowned in the river without pity,
dowsed with acid, sprayed with gasoline and then set on fire,
locked in their homes which were then set on fire,
to be propped up for bayonet drills,
hung by their tongues nailed to wooden boards,
to be mutilated, their faces pierced with needles,
ears hacked off, their eyes gouged out,
slivers of skin carved off, strip by thin strip,
penises cleaved off to be dried and consumed,
to be assembled together to be machine gunned
or to be blown up by hand grenades,
or one by one to be shot in the back by the side of a road,
to be stabbed, disemboweled, dismembered,
to be shoved into icy ponds, their frozen corpses
like floating logs used for target practice,
row upon row to be forced to kneel upon the shore
and then decapitated by swords slicing through necks,
severing flesh, crushing bone, their heads flying off,
torsos spurting twin fountains of blood,
crumpling into the mud, only to be dumped into the river
by the next row of men ready to take their places.

And then it was the women's turn.

THE NANKING SAFETY ZONE

Eyes red beyond tears
darting, filled with crazed hope
her voice so choked, past sobbing
past exhaustion and despair
that she can barely muster a whisper
her plea hoarse and deliberate
as she shoves through the ornate gate
through a narrow opening of cast iron
the bundle of her young son
just old enough to walk
but not yet weaned
wrapped tightly in a large padded jacket
a long scarf and woolen cap
squeezing him through the grating
into the surprised arms of strangers
those already crowded around camps inside
fortunate enough to have arrived earlier
inside the sanctuary walls
these walls shielding them from plunder and rape
the slaughter outside
even of infants bayoneted
or their heads dashed to the ground
in front of parents
an imaginable horror to this mother
now desperate to complete her last act
and then race away from the wall
vowing never to look back
as if it would be bad luck
her will so strongly focused
even against her own maternal instincts
that she could at all costs
care for him forever

but now she knows that this can never be so
and so for this one final chance
she takes control of her son's life
by giving him up
his survival with better odds than her own
a lone woman on the street
now unburdened and resigned
stealing away through the rubble of her wounded city
before the night that soon will come.

INSIDE HER WOODEN CHEST

My mother tells me to be brave.
She fears for me, a young girl.
When she goes out
I must hide inside her wooden chest,
the one she brought from her home,
when she got married.
It is a black lacquered box
with a simple lotus on the top
inlaid in mother-of-pearl.
She takes out all the clothes and blankets,
then spreads out one
to line the inside for me.
She gives me a knife
and shows me how from the inside
to slip it through the crack
between the top and bottom of the chest
until I can feel the latch
and push it open.
We practice this several times
so I know I can get out by myself.
But she says I should not worry
because she will return soon.
Before she leaves
she places inside the chest
a small ball of rice,
a jar of tea, and another jar
for me to urinate into.
She also makes sure
I see that she has put the lock
in the bottom of the chest
so that I do not feel trapped.
I climb in and she closes the lid,

folding the latch over its pin.
It is dark and quiet
though I can peek through the crack
and watch as the shadows
deepen into twilight, and into night.
I quickly learn that I can sit up
and extend my legs completely
if I push my feet against the far upper corners.
Sometimes I turn over
and crouch on my knees.
To while away the time
I add and subtract my numbers.
I think about the weaving I was working on.
I finish off the rice
and wait for my mother for a long time.
I fall asleep, curled up on my side.
I dream about the crickets my father kept
inside a small gourd cage
that he often carried in the palm of his hand.
I used to help him scrape the bottom clean
and replace it with new loam and lime.
It had an ivory top
carved through with five round holes
to allow for air.
I remember they sang so sweetly.

WE WATCH

our old donkey
being nailed from behind
by a draft horse.

How like a woman
braying pitifully
voice shedding tears

small feet
thin face
and elongated ears

bobbing up and down
her compact frame
sagging under the weight

rump giving way
at each thrusting
yet holding her ground

stubbornness
tinged with a sour smell
of transgression

warm fluids
trickling down
her hind legs

as if she does not know
what else to do
where else to go

except always
to suffer
our every bidding.

GOLDEN LOTUSES

"We'd never seen them before, so
we cut them off."
                    —in Honda Katsuichi,
                    The Nanjing Massacre

On the road next to a little bridge
a cone-shaped pile, knee-high,
with a single small foot at the top,
a very small foot as if a child's
and yet up close
it is wrinkled, gnarled, atrophied,
the four small toes curled underneath
growing back into the meat of the sole,
only the big toe remaining exposed,
an acute point,
like the shape of a baker's icing bag
or the prow of a small, slim boat,
except for the arch
which is raised, or rather buckled
into an unnatural ridge
where the length of the foot was broken
over the length of a lifetime,
the baby toe underneath
nearly touching the heel,
itself callused,
the shape of a fat mallet.

There are other feet,
some equally bare and shriveled,
others still in their shoes,
gaudily embroidered, even under the soles,
images of peonies and ducks in satin stitch,

appliqués of pink grapes,
a blue brocade of butterflies and chrysanthemums,
multicolored waves and tendrils,
a leaping fish with heavy silver couching.

The mound is stacked with care.
It is made from dozens of feet,
presumably all in pairs,
severed at the ankles or low shins,
encrusted now with blood,
exotic, once bound, but now freed,
now nowhere to run.

KANJI

ONNA
is the written character
for *woman*
depicting a figure
kneeling, crouching over
her arms hanging downward
crossed in front of her
demure
submissive
close to the earth

KAN
is written with three women
two on the bottom
and one on the top
like a pyramid
suggesting a noisy market
but this character
means *wickedness, treachery,*
seduction
—a sexual transgression

GO
is a character
composed of three parts:
a bow (as the radical),
privacy,
and a worm or insect;
together though
they make up the word
for *strong, violent,*
or *to force*

GOKAN
pairs the two characters
together
now forming
the word combination *rape*
as if with this act
the victim
perforce becomes
even more
of her true self

JUST PUNISHMENT

They broke into the temple
and mistook a monk

for a nun.
When they stripped off his robes

they discovered his penis
and became angry.

So they castrated him,
and held him down,

raping him as if a woman.
He had deceived them,

they all cursed.
He was not the woman

that they had imagined;
it was his just punishment then

to live out
the rest of his life as one.

AN AUTOPSY AT THE MOMENT OF DEATH

The big toe on the right foot
reveals a cut
from when she stubbed it
against a loose pile of rubble
as she was fleeing.
Scrapes on her knees, her elbows,
and the palms of her hands
show how hard she fell
when she tripped.
There are scabs on her scalp
above her left ear
where a clump of hair
was yanked off
as they caught up with her
and pulled her up.
Her skin is chalk white,
drained of color
in this winter light;
they ripped off her clothes,
leaving only one cotton shoe.
There are purple bruises
on her shoulders and upper arms
marking where they held her down.
Small rocks are imbedded into her back
around her shoulder blades
from when they pressed her
into the ground.
Her vocal cords are raw
from her screaming.
Her cheekbones bear red welts
where they struck her
to stop the screaming.

Two of her fingernails are broken off
from her frantic clawing
at their helmets;
some other nails, though, are unbroken
and contain underneath
traces of their skin
from where she scratched their faces.
Her pubic area is badly lacerated
from when they forced themselves
inside her one after the other.
The little finger on her left hand
appears pulled out of joint
as they pried away her ring.
The gash in her torso
on her left side
comes from the first of their bayonets,
a stab cracking her lower ribs.
There is a second wound
from a blade thrust into her groin
as she struggled to free herself
twisting about;
it punctured an artery
sending her into shock.
The pooling of blood underneath her
shows how she quickly bled to death.
She lies crumpled over,
her muscles slack,
her heart now stopped.
Only their sperm is alive,
moving within,
still furious and unrelenting.

IN THIS POSE

There is a sense of nonchalance in this pose,
two women basking in the sun
sitting against the side of a boulder
or a slant of earth;
a third woman to the left of them
is also lying against this incline,
but we can only see her from the side,
the bottom half of her body in this photograph.
The one in the center faces us squarely
though her head is slightly bowed.
The other has turned her head,
her lips somewhat pursed,
and looks over at the third woman
or at others beyond her whom we cannot see.
Their eyes seem to squint
as they face the sun, coming over
from behind the right side of the camera.

At least this is what I infer
because I cannot really see their eyes,
their hair and foreheads in shadows,
deliberately so, as the women are wearing shawls
or small pieces of patterned cloth
to shade the tops and sides of their heads
as protection from the sun.
Looking down I note that their shoes are black,
simple slip-ons made of cloth without arch straps;
instead, thin makeshift strips of ribbon
have been tied around the shoes
looping underneath the soles and over their arches.
More ribbon strips, their long bows dangling,
also keep their stockings up around their calves.

I had never realized that footwear was worn so,
but these feminine secrets have been bared
because that is all that they have on,
even for the third woman
(though it seems she may only be wearing stockings
or very light colored shoes).
They are stark naked otherwise,
and while today we are used to seeing
full frontal nudity in magazines and movies,
it is the very incongruity of this footwear
against this nudity, their exposed bodies,
which reminds me that they should not be,
for it is 1937, and in Nanjing, China.

These women like maybe tens of thousands of others
have been raped, maybe once, maybe dozens of times,
the rest of their clothes of no use anymore,
just their small breasts,
just their dark nipples against their pale skin,
just the plumpness of their bare midriffs,
the few wrinkles around their waists,
just the inward curving of their torsos
where the thighs meet, hinting of their clefts,
made even starker for the sparseness of public hair,
just their legs, white as jade in this winter light,
which, it is obvious, they have been told to spread.

And they do so in this glaring sun
without regard for any shame
for they are beyond such pornographic violence.
I discern no fear or horror in their expressions.
The woman in the center could be crying,
but it could as easily be her tired frown

merely welcoming the respite, I would guess,
savoring at least the fact
that they are still indeed alive.

These women would, though, still know
that, if he were like his comrades,
the cameraman, after raping them one last time,
would shoot or otherwise dispose of them inevitably
as just a few more cunts.
Except in his case it would not be before
he had captured them in this one last souvenir
with the shadow of his head protruding,
inadvertently, at the bottom of the photograph,
a ghost, a demon on the ground,
hell rising from beneath their feet.

THEY WERE MARKERS

"Extravagant defilements"
> —a euphemism found in a report by
> Menacham Amir, quoted in Susan
> Brownmiller, *Against Our Will*

They were told
to leave no
evidence. So just
as they burned down
storefronts after
lootings, they killed
the women after
their rapes—not with
bullets that could
be linked
back to them,
but with their knives
or bayonets. So
mass rape led
to mass murder.

But then why
did some leave
objects in the vaginas
of the dead? We
read eyewitness reports
of those who
found corpses
naked, or
at least with
their pants pulled
down, wooden rods,
twigs or weeds,

a stalk of cabbage,
a cane or broom, a golf
stick or a roll of
paper, perfume bottles,
beer glasses, bamboo
shoots, or even
a firecracker
protruding from
dark slits between
bare thighs,
jammed partly in,
yet obviously left
partly out,
deliberately, for
all to see.

They were markers, a
staking of
territory, evidence of
youthful pranks or
an inside joke
perhaps, something to
brag about to
each other as
to how ever more
creative each
new implement of
torture could
be, to give
pain and humiliation
to a woman as she
struggles to resist,
to rid herself
of impalement, this

intimate violation
knowing against hope the
obscenity of
being defiled forever.

A MOMENT OF THE TRUEST HORROR

They held
her down, inserted a grenade by
force, pulling
the pin just
before letting go
with one
well-aimed heel to
seal her
doom. Quickly they ran
for cover.

        She kneels
there, disheveled, bruised and
bleeding, unmercifully
undazed, eyes wide,
thighs pale, voice
quavering, shrill, all hands clawing
about; the belly wrenches,
ready to give
birth, at
this moment of the truest horror.

ON THE DAY BEFORE CHRISTMAS

She was the mother hen guarding all her chicks.
Thousands of Nanjing women, young and old,
sought refuge on her college grounds.
But the demons argued
that to protect these women
she must surrender one hundred prostitutes
for a licensed brothel—
in that way they claimed
their soldiers would not rape the rest.

It was a specious bargain.
She still protested, and they bullied their way in
calling out to all the refugees
huddled in the assembly hall
that they should not make matters worse,
that the professional women knew who they were,
that they did not belong in the school,
and they could make more money and be better fed
if they would volunteer.

Some stepped forward but not enough.
The missionary woman kept protesting,
denying that she sheltered any but decent women.
She would rather die than sacrifice
even one more girl.
The soldiers scoffed,
though it did not matter to them anyway.
They needed more—and decent or not,
it was still the same.

The missionary woman kept scolding the demons.
They fingered their bayonets,
prepared to grab the prettiest girls

closest to them.
Suddenly a well-respected gentleman,
a member of the Red Swastika Society
who had supported the college
and its efforts of resistance,
one who no one had ever thought
was familiar with such company,
stepped forward to appeal to the crowd
speaking in sweet words.
Enough women responded.
For once the missionary woman had nothing to say.

THE LESSON

"…the people kneeling at the side of the
road, Mary, Mrs. Tsen, and I standing, the
dried leaves rattling, the moaning of the
wind, the cry of the women being led out."
—Minnie Vautrin, diary entry for December 17, 1937

We enter noisily through the big gate,
demanding to see all the men.
We are looking for their soldiers who have deserted,
who buried their weapons
and threw away their uniforms.
This school has been turned into a refugee camp.
But it is being used to hide the enemy, we say.
We want to see the dormitories.
We want to see the storerooms and basements.
A few Chinese officials run out to stop us.
We slap them. We even slap
an old American woman who tells us she has no keys.
She seems to be the principal.
Still we search the school.
They keep saying nobody is hiding inside.
But it is a game; we know that they are lying.
We find a number of Chinese men.
We grab them, and they beg us to let them go.
We bring them to the gate, in front of our bayonets.
The woman says they are all cooks,
gardeners and servants,
other staff members who all belong here.
We order her to identify each one.
We bind them, and order them to kneel.
There are fifty men, they say,
so we warn them we will shoot anyone over that number.

After a while, three American men drive up.
After arguing with them, we force them away.
It is getting late, so we go;
we take one of the old teachers with us.
We are not followed, so we let him go
by the side of a burnt out store.
Now we are able to rejoin the rest of our unit.
They have been successful
sneaking in through the back of the school.
They have grabbed a dozen girls
during our distraction
—enough to keep us busy
for the rest of the night.

OUR MISSION

Wet Dream stood in front of me.
I turned around and squatted
so that he could climb onto my back
and sit atop my shoulders.
That way he could peek over the wall.

He turned around and grinned at us.
It confirmed the rumors we had heard,
what lured us to this foreigner's house,
so many families camping out,
seeking refuge in this garden.

We could hear the night murmurs
coming from the other side.
We could smell the stench
from their foul wastes.
It was as if the wall was alive.

So Wet Dream scrambled over the wall
with Gutless quickly joining him,
stepping onto Elephant's cupped hands
to be propelled upwards
like a slingshot to the top.

They disappeared down the other side;
soon we heard the commotion they caused.
This was our cue,
and we raced around the corner
to take advantage of their diversion.

Duck and Number 9 were waiting for us.
We helped them scale their wall as well.
After they dropped out of sight,
Elephant, standing watch, helped me up

so I could sit straddling the top.

All I could see in the moonlight
were dark bodies huddled here and there,
our flashlights scouring the shadows
to reveal their faces, white as death,
some dazed, some crying out.

Soon a girl with a shock of hair
was dragged close to the wall.
Quickly I pulled her up by her clothes,
then pushed her over to the other side
into Elephant's waiting arms.

Her feet were kicking,
her screams rising above the din,
so Elephant punched her several times
to keep her quiet.
She was a young girl around our age.

I brought my two buddies up
from out of the reach of the crowd.
Duck slipped off the wall onto the ground,
but Number 9 followed me
as I crawled along the top.

We looked around for our other buddies.
They were backed up against the wall
as if besieged by a swarm of ants.
A flashlight there moved back and forth,
violently, as if striking someone.

I yelled at the top of my voice
to tell them it was time to get out.
Suddenly a body wrapped in a blanket
was thrust up at us.

It was a white-haired woman whimpering.

We lifted her up, and then our buddies.
The old men and women jumped in vain
to try to pull us down.
A light was shone straight into my eyes,
a bright star blinding me.

All of us made it safely to the ground.
We found the first girl had snuck away
when Elephant and Duck left her
to help us down.
Still we had the older woman.

But Gutless had been hit hard,
his ear a bloody mess.
Someone had wrestled away his flashlight
and set about beating him.
We knew better than to retrieve it.

To make it up to Gutless,
we said he would have the first chance
to take the woman.
We retreated to our barracks,
our mission now complete.

SHADES OF WHITE

> "He remembered shades of white:
> skin, undergarments, snow."
> —Timothy Snyder, *Bloodlands*

Bare thighs shimmer
across the pond's surface
frozen over in the night.

The rent undergarments
flap in the icy wind
a clapper to a dirge.

Hair the color of frost
is cast about
as if emitting a scream.

But her eyes unflinching
harden into ivory
watching snowflakes fall.

WHITE TIGER

When the soldiers entered the city
my mother stopped two men on the street
and bought their shirts and trousers
for us to wear.
She sheared our hair short,
smeared soot on our faces,
and mixed in sticky rice and dirt
to darken our teeth.
She gave us canes to hobble with,
hunched over. But our new homeliness
did no good. They broke down our door,
raped my mother. My sister escaped,
but I was dragged to a brothel.

That first week I bled red,
the second week I bled red.
Thereafter, I bled white.
They told me now I was tainted
so no more tears.
They told me I was saving the honor
of other women in the city
so no more fists.
They told me my sacrifice
was good for soldiers' morale
so I should just lie back.
They told me that I was not dead
so I should be grateful.

They kept me naked day and night
reveling at the sight of my pale skin;
my only covering was a mosquito net
which I wrapped about me like a cocoon.

Later they found for me a kimono
of pert dragonflies, their wings
glittering like snow in the winter sun.
They gave me a foreign name
that reminded them
of flowers back home.
But they were in our country,
they were invaders.
Inside I was still pure
although every day they penetrated me,
my holes.

I was filled with disgust.
I thought I could outsmart them
and shaved my head bald
to disgust them even more.
Soon, though, it made me more popular
—the girl with no hair
whom they laughed at and scorned.
It gave them the idea
to shave my armpits,
eyebrows and pubic area.
I was their white tiger:
the more I fought
the more it gave them delight
in taking turns to break me.

As the months went by,
I indeed cared little for how I looked
lying in bed, waiting for them,
their curses, their ponderous bodies,
their thrustings.
I dreamed of my mother and her embroidery,
the nursery rhymes

my sister and I chanted,
the kite my father flew
that twirled with the wind
like a vermillion jewel,
that one day broke from its taut string
making good its escape.

The tide then turned.
We heard rumors of their flight.
Some soldiers wept with me in bed.
I did not pity them,
steeling myself for freedom's kiss.
Nor did I fear
that with one last act of violation
they would murder us all
to hide their crimes.
Death had passed us by too often.
I knew that I would survive;
it was to be my fate.

The war ended; I forgot the soldiers.
In my bath I scrubbed myself clean.
My appetite returned,
my body filled out.
My cheeks turned soft and ruddy.
I let my hair grow long and sleek.
I put on clothes the scent of persimmons.
Only I know they shroud
that abscess in my heart,
my well of shame.

THE BELT

Insert the tongue
into the metal buckle
and pull it through
almost all the way,
leaving a small loop,
enough room to slip in
a slender foot.
Cinch the belt
around the ankle.
Then from the other end
from one of the belt holes,
enlarged from constant use,
hang it onto a nail
hammered in at an angle,
at eye level,
to the post beside the cot.
This way this leg
is kept raised, straight up,
the knee unable to bend,
and the woman on her back
does not slide up,
her sex open,
always ready, all afternoon
and throughout the night.

NAKED

is all I wear
second nature now

stripped of shame
served raw

like their fish
translucent

a sheen of gold
this lure

of musk
and surrender

my brazen veil
to hide

from sight
the daily panic.

THE CHAIR

"The Kaneda Unit of the Army Field
Construction Company made this...after
my design"
—a caption accompanying
a photograph in Aso Tetsuo, *From
Shanghai to Shanghai*

I designed it
out of milled wood
cut and sanded clean
with an extra wide seat
raised to above table height.
On one side
two steps were affixed
so they could
easily climb on and off.
The board for the back
was set at a 45 degree incline
supported beneath
by long struts
reaching down to the floor
in order that
it would not tip over
when they reclined.
On the front edge
of the seat
I nailed on horizontal dowels;
this provided them
their knees bent
with something for their heels
to push against.
I had the front portion

125

of the seat
cut out in the center
so I could lean in closely
between their thighs
to check for sores
or telltale discharges.
I was not
on the front lines
but I was doing my part
to make sure
that those of us who were
were up to
their full fighting strength.

BEST ATTACK

"...the *Totsugeki Ichiban* condoms
were supplied by the maker, Kokusai
Rubber Company, as items of
standard military supply."

—Aso Tetsuo, *From Shanghai to Shanghai*

the city surrenders
   troops have time to rape
but they fear leaving evidence
   so they kill their victims too
so many women disappear
   the streets are empty now
the rest slip into hiding
   while invaders go unsated
the army must take action
   a war needs fighting men
they erect comfort stations
   where women serve day and night
the fuckings are relentless
   too soon bodies give out
diseases quickly spread to all
   doctors will join the fight
soldiers should be kept pure
   condoms are issued at the door
homeland factories are patriotic
   rubbers display their zeal
they imprint on each a battle cry
   one top brand is *Best Attack*

WONDER

Do demon
women who
work in
the rubber
factories back
in their
homeland ever
wonder why
so many of
the condoms
they make
must be
shipped to
our country
for use
by their
men on us?

INVIOLATE

The scent of sex
lingers like moonlight.
We lie on the cot,
I on my side, facing her,
she on her back,
her head turned towards the wall
away from the glare
of the lamp by the door.
My arm is snuggled
under her neck, our bare legs
hooked about each other,
entangled like eels in mud.
I can see her lifeblood pulsing
through the vein in her neck.
Her breathing slows,
barely perceptible, as a moth
alighting among dark leaves.
These past months
I have feared others' contact,
allowing no one,
not even my own buddies,
to get too close,
my skin, like glass,
ready to shatter.
I must defend myself
at all costs.
A bubble of air surrounds me,
an armor protecting me from harm.
Yet she is here,
with her shimmer of hair
electric against my cheek,
the sleek curve of her waist,

her thighs opened like a gift
—all within my grasp.
We do not speak
trying to preserve the silence.
There are no more bombs,
no rattle of machine guns,
no screams of agony
among the wounded,
just the two of us
in this small room, inviolate,
as I cling to her,
sequestered in my shadow,
as if this very moment
were our last.

LIVING-DEAD

"...even these most disposable
of commodity bodies were seen
to be indispensable for the
waging of total, imperialist war."
—Mark Driscoll, *Absolute Erotic, Absolute Grotesque*

My wounds bleed red.
My eyes shed sour tears.
My belly growls for food.
But they call me a toilet.
I am a mere receptacle
to give them release
for their excrements of lust.

I lard up my sex.
I open wide my legs.
I grit my teeth in silence.
But I serve as their robot.
My sole comfort is opium
—what they ply
to numb away my anguish.

I remember home.
I long to walk outside.
I dream of sleep.
But here there is only purgatory.
Even suicide is forbidden
as they grant us
no right to live or die.

CONDOMS

They gave us condoms
not because they wished
to protect us
but because they feared
they would catch our diseases.
But we had to serve
twenty of them a day
and many times
our supply ran out.
All we could do
for the next men
was to rinse out used ones
sticky with ejaculations,
their foul nectar.
They queued up
stripped of their uniforms
like plucked roosters
unwashed and unashamed
clutching their tickets.
As they put on their condoms
I coated my sex with lard.
This never helped though.
They were never gentle
even the young crybabies.
All they worried about
were their own ruttings
never the pain inside me
as with each thrust
each short grunt
I had to lie there
my legs splayed
upturned like a frog

exposing the belly
soft, pale white.
It was no wonder
as the months went by
that some of us got pregnant
when condoms gave out.
For a while
they kept us working
our wombs burgeoning
like boils.
They tried injections
to make us abort
but still a few gave birth.
I bore a boy
whom they then let me keep.
He was to be a part
of their great empire
a new recruit.
But then they lost the war.
We tried to go home
only everyone shunned us.
My son was proof
of my collaboration;
our enemy was in his blood
for all to see.

RAPES

"When gang-raped women in Konigsberg begged
their attackers afterwards to put them out
of their misery, the Red Army men appear to
have felt insulted. 'Russian soldiers do
not shoot women,' they replied."
—Antony Beevor, *The Fall of Berlin 1945*

1. Nanjing, 1937

The two of us broke open the front door.
Inside was all a mess.
Others had gotten there before us.
But in the attic huddled among some logs
we found a girl with close-cropped hair.
Quickly we stripped her bare.
Our lights blinded her, her eyes in a daze,
hands groping in front, to reach out,
or perhaps to ward us away.
She was a small slip of a girl, sallow skin,
with no breasts, no pubic hair.
I had never had someone so young,
but she turned out not much fun.
We only took a few moments.
She babbled on—I did not know what she said.
She smelled of fear, hugging the floor,
looking up at us
as if waiting to see what we would do next.
I pulled up my trousers, ready to leave,
but my buddy reminded me
that we were supposed to destroy any evidence.
So I picked up my rifle
and thrust the bayonet into her ribs.
She squealed like a pig for a long time

and then collapsed.
We returned to our unit,
and later that night I wrote in my diary:
We played fuck with a young girl today.

2. Berlin, 1945

The apartment building was badly damaged
but people were still living there.
I snuck inside and crouched under the stairs.
Soon a lone woman in a heavy coat
stepped into the entryway, carrying a bucket.
She wore her blonde hair in braids
which I grabbed, yanking her down,
face to the ground.
My hand was at her throat,
then covering her mouth.
The bucket, full of vegetables, clattered.
I hissed for her to keep silent.
She signaled her compliance with her eyes.
I reached under to tear away her underclothes,
baring her thighs.
Her body was pungent, unwashed.
It went slack; she did not move
—as if now resigned to let me enter.
The whole time her eyes followed mine
like a wary cat hidden in the shadows.
When I was done I stood up
and pushed her away.
Quickly I made my escape into the street,
into the safety of the sunlight
where my comrades were, ready for battle.

3. Congo, 1960

Two nuns, one old and one young,
were brought into our detention camp.
We forced them to take off their habits,
ignoring their pleas.
They seemed larger when naked,
with their pale skin mottled
as if covered with splotches of paste.
They squatted down, clutching their knees,
trying to cover themselves
with their waist-long hair.
We kicked them
and made them crawl on the ground like dogs,
sniffing each other's sex.
When we raped them they shrieked,
with eyes wild and frenzied.
One of them fainted;
we were not to kill them,
so we rushed over to revive her.
Afterwards we placed the two
in the pen with the others, naked as well,
hands tied behind their backs.
Some days other soldiers came in
and raped all the women there.
After a week, I could not tell
which of them were the nuns.

4. Bosnia, 1992

Our platoon was relieved,
and we were given a few days rest.
They bused us to a concrete building,
the basement of a sports hall,

a cave-like room bathed in fluorescences.
All told, there were five women
covered only in blankets
—plump pigeons in a coop.
Their faces were made up, some wore wigs.
We gathered around one or the other,
each to a mattress on the floor,
cheering ourselves on.
After finishing with the first
I moved over to another group to wait my turn.
We drank beer, we smoked, we slept,
we told jokes, we screwed again.
One of the women moaned the whole night,
one of them kept her eyes closed,
her teeth clenched.
Another threw up,
her vomit wafting through the hall.
What I remember most was the scar,
a long, thick welt,
running along the left side of one
from under her armpit down to her belly.
I wanted to have each of them
—but I got drunk and passed out.
We felt then we had all the power in the world.
It was a bloodlust with these women.
We would screw them
until they bore our children.
It was what we deserved.

5. Rwanda, 1994

I would bring out my machete for another hunt.
We sought out those cockroaches
scurrying in the fetid marshes.

When I caught them I would cut them clean
without so much as a glance.
Except for the young mother
who used to listen to the radio with us at home.
She was tall and slim,
and had smooth skin, our women said,
from always drinking milk.
She did not speak
but begged me with her eyes, full of tears.
I thought that anyway
she was marked for death,
so I took advantage of her in broad daylight,
roughly, her body prone against the earth,
my body on top of hers,
my fingers grasping at the roots of her hair.
But she did not scream out.
I told her if she wanted to keep on living
to come back to the same hiding place
on our next hunt.
We saw each other several times more.
I carried small sacks of food for her to eat,
always having sex, then letting her go,
to return to our hunt.
But my wife became suspicious,
others' tongues were wagging,
and I was not paying attention to her at night.
So one day I cut the woman,
quickly though, so she would not suffer.
More so than I, she knew it would not last.
I learned my lesson—
killing and fooling around do not mix.

AFTER OKICHI

August 28, 1945

After the two bombs were dropped
after we surrendered
after our Emperor sacrificed his divinity
the ministry prepared for the Devil's horde
—thirty women in simple kimono
orphans or widows of the war
none with experience
swearing fealty in front of the Imperial Palace
so like our young pilots just months ago
to dedicate themselves wholeheartedly
by offering their virtue
servicing the occupiers
in service of our country
preserving our good women
the purity of our race
this blood for our generations to come.

PART FOUR

"My mother's tears filled a small barrel."

PLUM BLOSSOMS

"Has the cold plum blossomed yet?"
—Wang Wei

Cold mountain winds scour the valley.
A hush descends upon the hard earth,

betraying no tears.
The gaunt plum hugs the river.

Its branches, shorn of leaves,
reach out like stark cries

in the winter night, a spider's agony.
Yet nubs of blossoms

nudge through the crinkled bark
on one twig, then another.

Buds nestle in crooks and crevices,
white as frost, grudging smiles,

a compassion nourished from within,
seeking air, seeking light.

A MARK OF OUR CIVILIZATION

"They must die that China can live."
—Madame Chiang Kai-shek, on the defense of Shanghai, 1937

It is said
that when their parents get old
eyes half blind
the hands too stiff to work
these invaders carry them
on their backs
to live in the mountains
where they soon die.
The children then
will have more to eat.

We have been nurtured
with tales of our forebears
who let children starve
in times of famine
especially those not yet weaned
whose cries are feeble
and who will not suffer long.
That way our elders
might live into their old age.
One can always bear another son,
but will never have another mother.
This hard choice
is a mark of our civilization
and is why
in the face of this war
we will nonetheless prevail.

HOW I AM TO END

After a skirmish
we would collect their dead
placing the corpses on top of firewood
which we also gathered.
They would wrap them in white shrouds
over which they poured kerosene.
A detail of troops would stand in a circle
surrounding the bodies,
solemnly, without speaking.
Then one of them would light
the shrouds in several places
to make sure that they caught on fire.
Everyone would wait
until the bodies were consumed,
and afterwards a few would pick through
the remains for the ashes and bones.
In turn these would be placed
in white kerchiefs to be tied
around the necks of their comrades.
This way even these invaders
would be able to return
to their motherland.

So different from how I am to end.
Kidnapped from my village,
I am forced to shoulder
their ammunition and food,
marching behind like a pack mule
until one day, exhausted, I will falter,
and they will think nothing of it
to stab me as I gasp for breath
by the side of the road,

of no use to them anymore,
my face hard on the ground,
blood oozing out,
a pain searing through my body,
crying for help, for their mercy,
against this rank indignity
of rotting away far from home,
far from my family,
who wait, unaware of my fate,
with nothing of me
but memories that are soon forgotten.

THEY

              eat coarse
rice and talk with
their mouths full. They rub
leaves together to wipe
their asses after
taking a crap. They
never bathe except
for the new
year. They blow
out snot straight from
their noses onto
the sidewalk. They drink water
brown with mud. They pick
over our trash as if
there were silver. They smoke
and swear and are
sullen all day. They work
only to get by and
pilfer on the side. How can
they say we treat
them badly when they
already live in
this squalor
of their own choosing?

THE COLLABORATOR

"If I could not be your sword,
I tried to be your shield."
—Petain

I was a radical too,
long before those who now continue to resist
were even born,
before they were even a glimmer
in their parents' eyes.
Famine relief, a home for orphans, the women's college
—they all know my generosity.

We are in perilous times.
Our nation is under siege.
These demons have already brought us to our knees,
their knives are at our throats.
One slip and we are all doomed.

Listen to me, we have to learn to accommodate,
to yield, to give in, at least on the surface.
Let the demons bring order to our country.
Think about it. That's better
than the chaos we had before they came.
All that bickering and bluster,
warlords in their petty cliques,
the shadow boxing that accomplished nothing.

Remember when we had to buy rice
with fistfuls of old money
—useless, even for toilet paper.
Remember the red gifts we had to bring
whenever we went into any ministry building.
That is why we are weak,

that is why we have been invaded.

The demons, we can negotiate with them.
Yes, it is another way to resist.
There may be those who have harmed us,
but they want to stop,
the soldiers and their leaders,
and I know so do we.

Let us stop the raping and protect our women.
Let us stop the looting
and provide security for our streets.
Let us stop the senseless killing
—if we show defiance, surely we will lose.

Look at how many tanks they have;
I would rather bow to them
as a small price to pay to preserve the peace.
I want to save whatever we have left,
certainly that is still more than what we have lost.

This is not the time to engage in lofty words.
Let us roll up our sleeves.
If a man has fallen and hurt his head,
we must first stop the bleeding
—forget about who pushed him
or whether we must fix the road.

We cannot save the whole world,
we cannot save this whole country,
but at least save your own family
—you have that responsibility.
I have a family, they are what I care about most,
and I am sure you do too.
For their sakes, we should all work together.

THIS REASONING

"Although there is nothing wrong with this
reasoning, yet as soon as I heard it, I
cried. I thought my own country is not
strong, so it suffers this kind of
humiliation. When can we shed the shame?"
— Tsen Shui-fang, diary entry for December 19, 1937

TEACHER: Your buildings have filled up quickly, I see.

NURSE: Yes, even though we restricted our campus to
only women and children, thousands have come
to find refuge in these last few days. Too
bad some families have had to decide to split
up or together they get turned away.

TEACHER: Outside, every day is blacker than the day
before. We have seen men on the road tied
together with ropes around their waists being
dragged away. We have listened to women
standing in the backs of open lorries crying
out to anyone who can hear for help.

NURSE: This safety zone may be the only way to protect
them. But even here, morning and night, the
demons force their way through our gates and
scale our walls to kidnap even more. We are
like a small boat leaking in a sea of blood.

TEACHER: But I came to ask you to send back the married
women so they can return to their husbands at
home.

NURSE: Why would you ask that?

TEACHER: Not the young girls. Only the wives. When
                the demons break into a home, if they find
                only a man there, they think that he is one of
                our deserter soldiers hiding out, since he has
                no family. So then they take him away.

NURSE: But if the wives go home, the demons will push
                the husbands out so they can rape the wives.
                Do you really want one sex to sacrifice their
                bodies for the other? When a fox comes, why
                must we have to choose between the rooster and
                hen?

OUR ACTRESS

"Then, she went inside to change
clothes…This person is really admirable."
—Tsen Shui-fang, diary entry for December 29, 1937

"Quick! Quick!" she exclaims, and she pulls
on my arm. We bound upstairs to the room
we share with three others. Immediately she
starts taking off her dress and shoes. I look
at her dumbfounded. She hisses at me. "Quick!
Give me your dress, the green one!" She is
referring to the one I keep in my trunk,
which I take out only for special occasions.
As I rummage through my clothes, I ask,
"Why do you want my dress?" She tells me,
"I need to change into it now to go back down
to get another one." She has already claimed
some sullen, bald-headed man as her father.
She pulled him out of the crowd of those whom
the invaders suspect as our soldier deserters,
of those who if no one identifies them will
disappear forever. Now, he waits in the shadows
of our vestibule. "How do you think you
will be able to get away with this one more
time?" I challenge her. She looks at me
with her wild, sparkling eyes. She
finishes buckling her shoes, and stands up
straight—pausing to let me look her over. She
is a head taller than me, so the hem
falls only to her knees. I observe, "Luckily
we have been starving these past few weeks,
so now you have lost enough weight to fit
into my dress." She smirks. Deftly she dabs

on lipstick and rouge that she finds in the box
of one of our roommates, and then grabs a floral
shawl from another to cover her head. We race
down the stairs and out the doors. So many
men are still lined up, and without hesitation
she rushes over, wailing loudly, to where
the trucks are. "I found you!" she cries out,
flinging her arms around a stocky young man
hunched over. She kisses him several times,
and he starts to sob as she pulls him back to
our side of the road. We engulf the two
of them. She is still calling him "Husband" as
we lead them into the courtyard. Later,
we gather together with her "family." They tell
us that they are not soldiers and were rounded
up in the dragnet. The younger one has a wife
and child, and will now return to them;
the older man is not from here and plans to
leave the city as soon as he can. We wish
them well, as our actress wipes away the smudges
of lipstick from the young man's cheeks.

WHAT THE INTERPRETER SAW

"They indeed lost…face totally. It
made me angry to death."
—Tsen Shui-fang, diary entry for January 2, 1938

We escort three demon women
to the refugee camp
to celebrate the new year.
In their fur-lined coats
and sleek leather boots
they pass out dried apples
and hard candy in pink wrappers
to the assembled children.
Some of the rag-clad mothers
press around them, loud,
jousting, arms outstretched,
hands grasping for the candy,
small coins, or anything
to fill their empty palms.

The owlish nurse in spectacles
who brought the families
starts hissing at the mothers,
scolding them for their commotion
(she knows that the demons
cannot understand her).
She calls them
ignorant and without shame,
saying they should rather starve
than display so brazenly
our continuing desperation.

But these unseemly women
are just trying

to feed their families,
snatching just one extra sweet
to carry their children through
just one extra day—
so hopefully they can grow up
to decide for themselves
when it will be
important to save face
and when it is
all right to lose it.

WE DO NOT NEED TO ASK

She says a demon officer
expressly paid a visit
requesting that we take in
a young woman
and her younger sister.
He is leaving
for the front soon
and knows how our shelter
protects refugees.
How impressed she is
that even our enemies
display such concern
for women still on the outside.
But when the two show up
in a private car
we are taken aback.
They wear bright lipstick
and bring brand new coats
and heavy quilts,
and a leather satchel
filled with tins of food.
They readily admit
that they have been staying
at the officers quarters
for over a month.
What work these young women
have been doing
we do not need to ask.
Several other refugees
start cursing them,
and I am hard pressed
to tell them to keep quiet.

A GAME WE ALL PLAY

They come to inspect
and to cajole. They claim
that order has been restored
and that the rest of the city
is now safe for us
to send our refugees
back to their homes.
They post notices for us
to close our camp. We must
take down all of our tents;
otherwise they will dismantle them
by force. We keep delaying
the day. We tell them
it is snowing or perhaps
that the older women
can return first
—we want to hold off
on the younger women and children.
We promise that we will have
everyone dispersed
but never say when.
So they keep up
their inspections.
                        Each time
they visit they bring along
the same interpreter
who says the same thing. We smile
and give him the same response
to tell them. It is
a game we all play.
But it is not, he tells us
soberly. He takes us aside

156

and whispers to never
trust them. He is one
of our soldiers
whom they captured. He goes
with them everywhere and can see
everything. Outside, many houses
have been looted
and torched. Corpses still lie
on the roads, and women, raped.
His tears well up; he plans
to escape. We must stay
where we are. This is all
the home we have,
and we can never leave it.

HE WOULD BEAT

me with his slipper as I tried
to squirm away, striking me
on my shoulders, or the back of my head,

just for returning
late from the market.
When I spilled my bowl

of soup at the dinner table,
he called me over
to stand in front of him, to stick out

the offending hand, palm up,
to receive the whack
of his chopsticks. If I talked back

to him, he would squeeze
my arm hard, until
I yelped. If I got too bored

massaging him in the mornings,
he would crack
his knuckle on my forehead.

So when the demon
soldiers came and slapped
my father's face for not bowing

to the officer, I secretly said
good for him. Everyone
will taste the power of another someday.

A POT OF RICE GRUEL

They marched the father away by the collar
to wash their uniforms the whole day,
tall tubs of hot, soapy water,
leaning over a washboard scrubbing shirts,
wringing out puttees to dry.
He knew he should be grateful;
others he had heard had never returned.
And he brought back a small sack of coarse rice.
So in the setting sun, his family of six
all squatted around the fire next to their tent
waiting for the rice gruel to boil down.
A passing soldier approached
pushing aside the wife.
He unbuttoned his trousers,
letting go a stream of piss into the cast iron.
The demon said nothing
as if just concentrating his aim,
a glint in the dying light.
Neither did the family, even the children,
their faces flickering against the night,
just staring wide-eyed, some mouths agape,
as if no one could breathe,
the moment before tears would well up.

THE SCAVENGER

"In the nightmare of the dark
All the dogs of Europe bark"
—W. H. Auden, "In Memory of W. B. Yeats"

Squat, short-haired cur, fur
a smudge of dirty white, a stub
of tail erect, snub snout picking over the arm,
rooting out the flesh, gnawing bone.
She senses my approach
and turns about to face me, head cocked
to one side, ears
pricked, eyes alert, wary, careful
to stand her ground between me
and the slain soldier. Safeguarding
her meal, she must be as famished
as we are. But I am revulsed and chase her
down the lane, past the rubble
and burnt-out houses, until I can grab hold
of her leg. She claws the air
and snaps at me, so I fling her
against a brick wall
stunning her long enough
to truss her up, carry her to the butcher
where I sell her. I take the cash though
—she has human flesh now
in her blood, so I turn down
the butcher's offer of a fresh haunch
as part of the spoils.

A SOLDIER'S REPORT

The teenager is tall
and bamboo-thin. We catch him
trying to crawl away
when we start clearing out the rubble
of a bombed-out temple.
He does not get very far.
His clothes are tattered. He smells
of death. So many
maggots are already trying
to find a way to enter
his body, swarming around his nose,
his ears, his mouth.
We sit him down and take
a long time to get him to drink
a few sips of water. He keeps saying
thank you in a mosquito-like
voice. Although his face
is dark with grime,
his hollow eyes still
shine as bright as morning.

THE RICE

was yellow, unhulled,
and as hard as the round jar
this cache was hidden in
when we discovered it
buried behind an abandoned house
already foraged over
by many others before us.
We were surprised
to have come across it,
and just seeing it
reminded us of our hunger.
We had hardly eaten in days
and could not wait,
but we had no matches,
no pot, no wood for a fire,
no water to boil.
We could only think
to use the jar,
its surface metallic and smooth,
to grind down the grains
on a sheet of newspaper
we laid out on the stone floor.
We started crushing
some twenty kernels at a time,
loosely spaced.
I rolled the jar,
pressing down hard,
my wife and young son
cupping their hands
around the sides
to keep any fragments
from flying away.

In time we built up
a small mound of coarse powder,
the size of a fist.
My wife was the first to taste it
taking a pinch
and with a quick smile
declared it ready to eat.
I lifted the newspaper
and poured a small stream
of this rough mash
into our boy's outstretched hands,
cautioning him to chew slowly.
He could not help but laugh
at the crunching sound
he kept making.
Later we took turns with the jar,
even my son
though his pudgy fingers
soon tired of the work.
We took our time with this meal,
until we had had our fill.
Our son licked his palms clean,
and we exited the gate
grinning and content
carrying the empty jar
—our souvenir.
It did not matter
that in the evening
each of us suffered
from bloating and cramps.
We had made it
through one more day.

HUNGER

We had been hungry even before the demons came,
my sister, cousin, and I, living day to day,
stealing cotton scraps at the go downs,
sweeping the wooden planks of the piers,
crouched over like snails,
for loose grains of rice or flecks of coal.
After the city fell we found the home
of a family who we knew had been killed.
We slept in the attic by day
coming out only at night
when the soldiers finished their marauding,
to sneak into abandoned houses and stores,
scavenging cellars of those who had escaped.
We discovered caches of rice, cans of peaches,
salt fish wrapped in waxpaper under a mattress,
sunflower seeds, and pickled cabbage.
But we still envied another family
who bragged they had unearthed two antique vases
which they exchanged for a live chicken.

As the days went by, however,
food and water became scarce.
We took to rationing our fuel,
cooking only once each night just before dawn.
But we were easily fatigued,
some days too sluggish to go out to forage.
All three of us were losing weight,
our cheeks hollowed out, shoulders slouching,
our eyes retreating into our sockets
like shriveled black mushrooms.
Our abdomens flattened
—we became like the young girls we once were.

164

But our insides were betrayed by an empty ache
as if unable to hold up the organs within.
Later, my sister rising from her morning bed
would sometimes urinate down on herself,
much to her embarrassment,
her muscles uncontrollable, loose as tofu.

Then at dusk one night
our cousin, the youngest and strongest of us,
ventured outside by herself
vowing to return with her arms full.
But by sunrise she had not.
We waited and prayed, but knew without saying
that she must have been kidnapped, or worse.
Suddenly, there were only the two of us left,
my sister and me—paper and scissors
but without the stone.
Without her, the savor of life slipped away,
steamed buns now stale, crumbling into thin air.
We had one less mouth to feed,
but we still cut our daily portions once again,
hoping to just hang on.
We hardly left the house,
our night soil accumulating for days.

We had run out of food,
and my sister became bedridden.
Her feet swelled up like plump sausages,
her skin so painfully taut,
shining in the candlelight.
Even so we found delight
in sharing each other's recipes
—savoring her favorite scallion pancakes,
my dumplings filled with chicken and chives,

the jellyfish and cold bitter melon.
But she knew she would be dying soon.
She called me over whispering hoarsely in my ear
making me swear to eat her body whole
after she was gone.
That way both of us would then survive,
and her suffering all these days
would not have been in vain.

Indeed she died the next day;
my eyes could shed no tears.
I laid her out, her pallid face up,
her arms and legs mere skin and bones
—dried bean curd sticks, wrinkled and brittle.
I bit into her thumb, to honor my promise,
breaking her skin to draw out her blood,
so thin and pale and slightly bitter,
sucking it out like a straw
—our one last long kiss.
It was enough sustenance for me.
Drained of her soul, death weighed her down.
I had no way of burying her body
so I left her and moved down to the kitchen.
Just to keep warm I broke up the furniture,
piece by piece, for kindling wood for the stove.

There was nothing to do
but sit and listen to the world about me.
Rats scurried in the attic, and my heart leaped,
but I could not bear to go up there again.
Outside, I could hear the occasional explosions,
sometimes the shooting, sometimes screams.
My tongue felt rough, my lips sore and puffy.
Red spots appeared on my skin.

I was listless and short of breath.
Only then did I realize
that I had missed my monthly bleeding.
It was as if my body was preserving itself
husbanding my lifeforce,
like small animals in wintertime burrowing in.
I huddled in my woolen coat,
and told myself I would outlast this war.
I kept my eyes open and waited for the spring.

WHERE WE LEFT OUR FAMILY

"There was nothing we could do. We
were helpless…and walked away."
—Luo Daxing, then seven years old

We were discovered in the forest.
They shot our mother and our elder cousin.
I was hiding in a ditch filled with mud.
After they left, I ran over to them.
Our cousin did not move;
our mother was silent,
but her left hand trembled, reaching for the sky.
She did not speak, her face full of blood.
Later, she stopped moving.

I gathered up our bottle of cooking oil,
the green kerchief and the comb.
These were all that we had managed to escape with.
My sister clutched me tightly and did not let go.

I started to walk away.
Another sister who was just a baby
had been circling our mother.
She tried to follow us, but also wanted to stay.
She could not keep up.
I thought with one sister hanging on to me
I could not carry the baby too.
I would not have been able to run.

We walked away faster to shake her off.
Soon she turned back to where our mother lay.
Moving on, we found a shelter with rice inside,
but we had no matches to make a fire.
So we went to sleep.

The next morning my sister said
we should return to our mother
—that maybe she would be awake.
She did not understand that our mother had died.
I did, but I hoped secretly
that she might have come back to life.

She had not, but our baby sister was there
lying on top of her.
She had opened my mother's blouse to suckle.
When we arrived, she was still alive
and raised her stubby arms towards us.
But she was very weak.

There was nothing we could do,
so we walked away again.
We walked back to the shelter
and then to a village which we found was abandoned.
My sister said again
that we should go back to our mother.
I hoped our baby sister was still alive.

But she was not—
although she was where we left her,
on our mother's breast.
She was now cold to the touch
and she did not move.
We were very sad and sobbing, went away again.

At dusk we came upon two men
whom we brought to the shelter.
They had matches and cooked the rice
for all of us to eat.

The next day we were about to follow them
but troops chased after us.

We ran off in a different direction.
Not knowing where to go,
the two of us made our way back to our mother.
It was sunny and warm.

Soon three villagers found us
and buried our elder cousin,
our mother and baby sister.
We stayed with one of the men
who later adopted my sister and me.
We changed our surname
and still live not far from the forest
where we left our family.

ESCAPING THE WAR

My mother's tears filled a small barrel.
It was all I could carry
when we fled the capital.

Some people found passage down the river,
while others followed
our soldiers along the road west.

We took to the hills
wending our way through steep gullies
full of dry leaves.

The barrel grew heavy.
I feared I could not keep up
and hugged it with all my might.

At night we rested near the edge of a clearing.
As I dreamed, the moon burned through the barrel
turning the tears into molten gold.

I could hear the sounds
of shouts and weeping from within.
Our keening echoed throughout the night.

In the early dawn I tried to lift the barrel.
But it had sunk into the hard winter earth,
much heavier than before.

I pried open the top
scooping up whatever fistfuls
I could manage, and quickly slipped away.

We passed through abandoned farms, hid in forests,
but avoided ridgelines
where we might be spotted by airplanes.

We reached a camp and then another.
Later, we scattered,
disappearing into towns and small cities.

Throughout the rest of my life
I have held on to the pocket watch
that was made from the gold.

It has kept its shine all these years.
Every day I open its cover;
I am filled with sorrow's scent.

It tells me the same time
no matter what
—December 13, 1937, Nanjing, China.

HAIR

Deserters were betrayed by callouses and crew cuts.
So he hid his head under black fungus and a shawl,
hobbling out a city gate in a slack dress.

The intruder yanked her up from under the bed
by the clutch of her hair;
she feared her torn scalp would never heal.

With her largest scissors
the seamstress sheared off her granddaughter's pigtails
to disguise her sex.

The family hid in the basement,
but their store was looted and then put to the torch.
They all raced out, hair in flames.

The officer wore spectacles and grinned ear to ear,
his sword in his right hand,
his left dangling a severed head by its hair.

Her gray robe, false teeth and bald head
were of no protection
to ward off the old nun's rape.

The mistress found a photo of his sister in a knapsack;
as a surprise she permed her bangs in the same style
so that the captain would be reminded of home.

Wanting a souvenir of his conquest,
the corporal chopped off the student's thick tresses
with his blood-stained bayonet.

Lice were prevalent in the brothel.
All the prostitutes' heads were shaved;
wigs with curls became the rage.

Her hair was like silk, ink-black, and fell to her hips.
But they were hungry, so her husband sold all of it
to the invaders for their wives back home.

They found a mass grave—
bodies jammed one against the other, still clothed,
decomposing, hair matted to flesh.

An interpreter's girlfriend was kidnapped.
The resistance wanted to punish consorters
and clipped off her hair as a warning to others.

Joining the guerrillas,
the farmer's daughter kept her hair cropped close;
patriots were no different when it came to women.

I WILL STILL

Even if they gouge out my eyes
I will still see the bayonets thrust into my son.

Even if they slice off my ears
I will still hear the screams of the nurses being raped.

Even if they crush my nose
I will still smell the rot of our neighbors' corpses.

Even if they pull out my tongue
I will still taste the blood staining our wells.

Even if they peel off all my skin
I will still feel the heat from our homes burning.

Even if they chop off my legs
I will still walk though our looted streets.

Even if they break my arms
I will still clutch our dead teacher to my breast.

Even if they cut off my head
I will still know the evil that swells their hearts.

UNRIGHTEOUS

OFFICER: Who are you?

MAN: I found you!

WOMAN: Why are you here?

MAN: I finally found you!

OFFICER: Stop! What is all of this?

WOMAN: How did you get here?

MAN: I had to pay off people to learn where you were.

WOMAN: Pay people? With what?

MAN: With this gold. I sold our furniture. I sold our house. All for this gold. Except for what I had to pay the middlemen, this is what I have been able to bring.

WOMAN: Why did you do this?

MAN: Others said that they saw you here. I had thought you were already dead. I was so ashamed.

WOMAN: So now what do you want to do?

MAN: Please take this gold. She is my wife. Please let her go.

OFFICER: You want to buy her?

MAN: She is my wife. Please let her go. I can give you all of this.

OFFICER: We took her. But for this gold, you can have her.

WOMAN: What? No!

MAN: Why?

WOMAN: Why would I want to go back to you?

MAN: I came all this way here to get you. Look how heavy this bar is. Here, take it all. I want her back.

WOMAN: No!

OFFICER: All this gold in exchange for you.

WOMAN: No! Now he has nothing. If he gives you all this gold, what do we have left? Now we have no home. I do not want to live as a beggar on the streets. I would rather stay here with you.

MAN: How can you say that? At least we would be together.

WOMAN: You fool! Who would want to live with you? Even before, when we were at home, we had so little money, even less food, never enough heat. I have suffered enough already.

MAN: Ungrateful!

WOMAN: Here this man takes care of me. He protects me. Look at this new coat. See how fat my cheeks are now. What can you do?

MAN: Then what everyone has said is true.

OFFICER: So you will not go?

WOMAN: No. Never again. Not even if you paid me this gold.

MAN: Have you no face? If not for yourself, then for me?

OFFICER: I feel sorry for you. Now you know what kind of woman you have.

MAN: I should never have come.

OFFICER: We took you by force. You had no choice then. But now you do. You have been a comfort to me, but at some point we will move on, and I may not be able to bring you along. Are you sure you do not want to go back with him?

WOMAN: I am. I wish to go with you.

MAN: What kind of wife are you?

OFFICER: Do you want her back now?

MAN: She is married to me. But no, not now. I thought you were dead. Now you truly are.

OFFICER: Then let me return this gold back to you. You may leave now. I will have someone make sure you get back safely.

MAN: I see. Thank you. So you will keep her?

OFFICER: She is an unrighteous woman. She is not worthy enough for you. Or for me.

WOMAN: How can you say that? Have I not shown my appreciation?

OFFICER: I do not want you either.

WOMAN: Have you not enjoyed me?

OFFICER: For a time, yes. It was because you were resistant that kept me attracted to you. But not anymore.

WOMAN: Who then is really ungrateful?

OFFICER: Remember, I can send you someplace where you cannot refuse anyone.

WOMAN: Let me be. I will take care of myself. I have done what I needed to survive. But I will not be anyone's possession anymore.

OFFICER: Go back with your gold. You are better off. We are both better off without her.

WOMAN: It is easy to speak about what is right or wrong when you carry the sword or a fistful of gold. Yes, I too am better off without the two of you.

AS USUAL

I was peeking through the bushes.
The sisters, the prettiest girls in the valley,
were washing clothes by the bend in the river,
and after wringing their garments dry
they slid into the water themselves,
as usual, fully clothed.
This was my special moment
to see them bathing, frolicking in their privacy,
their bare calves glistening,
their long loosed hair
swirling about the water's surface,
their voices carrying aloft
sweet village tunes.
                              But this one day
a collaborator from town passed by.
He motioned to them to go over
to the path where he was standing
and then grabbed the oldest by the arm
as if to take her away.
Her younger sister was pulling on her other arm,
pleading with him.
I did not know what to do.
I wanted to come out to stop him,
but then everyone would find out
that I had been spying.
                              Suddenly
the elder sister let out a loud shriek,
and without thinking I bolted out
calling to the man to release them.
I told him about the rest of the women
who were hiding in the bamboo forest
and that I knew where they were

and would take him to their shelters.
He asked me many questions
and seemed interested enough
that he let the sisters go.
They quickly backed away
and huddled together near the river's edge
but did not say anything.
                  I led him
across the river, skipping over submerged rocks.
He followed me as best he could
but tried too hard and slipped and fell.
I had already made it to the other side,
but he was stranded in the middle,
not knowing whether to continue or to go back.
In either case, he did not know the way,
the path underwater being hard to see,
and asked me where it would be safe
for him to cross.
              Without hesitation
I pointed over to the quiet pool
enshrouded by the overhang of the old banyan.
He took one step and sank immediately
for that was where we all knew
the river bottom dropped off.
His body remained submerged,
the only part of him left was his hat,
which floated to the promontory,
and which I promptly buried.
                  I returned
to where the sisters were,
kneeling on the shoal of the river.
They did not know whether to laugh or cry
but offered salt plums for me to eat.

All they said was
that I did not have to crouch
behind the thorns as usual.
I could help them carry their bundles
every washday from now on.

THE CHINESE VIOLIN

The looters broke down the door.
The family was huddling in the cellar,
faces ghost white.
Their rice was seized,
the cash hidden in a broken teapot,
a prized pocket watch, gold bracelets and pins.

Some ordered the mother to feed them.
Others stripped her daughter, a tall teenager,
as she bleated like a doe
brought down by tigers.
The captain found an *er hu*, a Chinese violin.
He asked who in the family knew how to play it,
and the father stepped forward.
He was instructed to sit in the middle of the room
on a three-legged stool,
the two-stringed instrument upright on his lap,
to entertain the soldiers as they ate.
He was hesitant, his family all in tears.
The officer told them to keep quiet
and, irritated, ordered the father to play;
if he stopped, he would then be shot.

The father wiped down the silk strings,
his hands could not keep from trembling.
He played terribly, shoulders stooped, sobbing
as he clutched his horsehair bow.
For some reason, as if by rote,
he chose a cheery tune—
mandarin ducks splashing in a stream.
It was a happiness he could not swallow.

But soldiers in the corner became bold,

were raping his daughter.
His wife and young son dared not to move,
bayonets pointed at each of them.
The girl was screaming,
as if claws were thrust into her,
blood seeping onto the floor where she lay.
The father beseeched the soldiers but kept on playing.
The captain, annoyed, warned him not to stop.
The playing continued, the raping continued.

The father was bawling, an ox sensing its slaughter,
drowning out his melody.
The captain yelled at the father.
Those men will stop whenever you do, he sneered.
The father cried out, asking
if he was a man of his word. The officer nodded.

The father immediately let go the bow,
his right hand opened and raised.
The silence stunned the soldiers and family alike,
as if caught in the typhoon's eye.
The officer collected himself,
pulled out his pistol
and shot the father in the heart.
The violin fell to the ground. His wife blanched.
His stool was splattered with blood.
Only the soldier raping the daughter continued,
grunting, a rutting pig, oblivious to the thunderclaps.

The daughter kept wailing.
The captain, pistol in one hand,
yanked up her attacker with the other.
His pants floated down around his ankles.
The captain at close range discharged a bullet
straight into the soldier's heart,

blood pooling about the girl,
her stark pale skin.
He had given his word as an officer.

The two men lay dead on the floor
like discarded grains of rice.
The captain breathed calmly,
motioning his men to eat.
He had killed so many more than this.
He wondered out loud
what made that man so foolish
as to sacrifice his life.
He beckoned the young son over
and told him to play.
He told him also to keep on playing
and that whenever he stopped his mother would die.

The boy was only a beginner
but, composed, picked up the Chinese violin
resolving to do his best.
Perched erect on the stool, he played a simple tune,
arduously, over and over and over;
it was the only one he knew.
It described a proud phoenix soaring.
His sister lay in the corner exhausted and dazed,
his mother swooning with grief.

The boy plied his bow back and forth.
Soon his untrained fingers became cramped.
After each repetition he faltered,
the song turned into a dirge.
Soldiers smirked, flicking their bayonets.
Suddenly the mother lunged forward
into one of them, piercing her heart.

She died instantly,
a hen protecting her chicks.
The boy dropped the violin
and rushed to her to try to revive her,
his palms smeared in blood.
A soldier grabbed him by the collar;
others circled around prepared to pummel him.

But the boy's sister ran over to their captain
appealing to his honor
as an officer of the imperial army.
She said their mother was now dead
and begged forgiveness for the boy.
The officer took a deep breath, and agreed.

Only his men yearned for more blood.
At least one of these people
should eat bitterness, the sergeant said.
The officer made the two children
fight for the violin.
Whoever got to play it first
would be killed, and the other released.
In the middle of the room
the sister and brother stared at each other,
each holding fast to the violin, for a long time.

All at once they threw it on the ground,
stomping it like a cursed rodent,
crushing its neck and sound box.
Tuning pegs careened across the floor.
The girl picked up the bow
and broke it over her knee, the bamboo splintering.
They turned to face the soldiers surrounding them,
back to back like sticky beans,
the brother breathing heavily, anxious,

the sister still naked and flushed,
her bare feet cut and bleeding
—a standoff until the captain stepped in between.

He glowered at the children.
The sister coolly reminded him of his promise.
Neither sibling had won the Chinese violin,
so neither should be killed.
The money and jewelry were never returned.
The soldiers carried out the remaining rice
and their dead comrade.
They filed out of the house led by the captain,
leaving the children and their mourning behind.

AFTER SIX WEEKS

Even the stallion
after lightning thrusts
will slip off his mare
sweaty, in a victorious huff
their frenzied imperative spent.

Even the typhoon
after ravishing the forests and fields
will release the sky
still in shock
drained of all weight, clear.

Even the army
after its fevered sack of this city
will pause to cheer, white arms raised
a bloodlust sated
now ready to do battle again.

PART FIVE

"…ragged lines across a sun-drenched sky."

THE PROFESSIONAL MOURNERS

When the bombs
began to drop
our business increased.
We performed at funerals
several times a day,
wailing over an elder
sobbing for a child
so often
clutching the caskets
beseeching the dead
not to leave us so soon.
But the invaders
broke through
our city gates.
Men were beaten
and slain on the streets,
women were raped
and murdered
in their homes.
There were not enough
mourners to hire
for each burial.
We had hardly any time
to take off
our white headbands
and clothes.
Day to day
we lived through
a cacophony
a suona played
without tunes.
Neighbors went missing

their bodies never found.
Corpses of strangers
appeared everywhere,
but no one
knew their names.
Mass graves were dug
in the mountains,
their souls jumbled together
trapped deep in the earth.
No one wept over
a single death anymore.
Everyone had exhausted
their tears,
too overcome
with constant grief.
Our voices quavered.
For the first time
we feared death
for ourselves.

THIS MORNING: A LOVE POEM

"...or watching a bird leap from the edge
of the rooftop"
—Dorianne Laux, "How Will It Happen, When"

He wipes up the shavings inside his basin.
On the floor next to her chair lie loose strands
of her long dark hair. He neatly folds his blanket
and rolls up the mattress. Already her top sheet
has been stacked with her extra pillows

in the far corner. As he passes by the bookshelf
he takes note of the pile of composition books,
student homework which she has corrected;
he smiles and walks to the dresser,
to where he has been mulling over an editorial

which he started to write out on a clean sheet
of paper. At the birdcage he changes a spray
of millet for his finch. The old tobacco cans
filled with her garden of coriander and green onions
crowd the windowsill, newly watered and turned.

Her tin of tea leaves, especially picked
in early spring, has been placed back on their table.
From the ceramic pot beside it he ladles out
leftover soup, now reheated, taking sips from a bowl
he holds with both hands. Hung to dry

on the bamboo pole outside the window,
her underthings nudge against his, their shirts
embrace in the gentle breeze, their pants entangle.
His world will continue its inexorable revolutions,
even as this morning her days will now end.

ALL HER LOVE FOREVER

She lays him down carefully
on his side of the bed
where he usually sleeps
on his right, knees bent
cheek resting upon a pillow.

She squeezes in beside him
in between him
and the close edge of the bed
her stomach snug
against the small of his back.

Her thighs scrunch in under his;
with the shorter reach of her legs
her feet wrap around
grasping his shins
as if never to let go.

She slips her right arm
crooked under his neck
her left hand in a fist
pressed into his chest
her chin hooking into his shoulder.

Her moist breath curls about his ear
a salt fragrance.
Her heart beats like a small bird
the warmth of her skin
fresh and tingling.

Under moonlight her long loose hair
shimmers like a shawl
enveloping them.
It is as if all her love forever
could just bring him back to life.

EVEN OUR BONES

are scraped of flesh, immersed
in lye, bleached and dried,
cracked open over a slow fire,
brittle edges turned to ash,
marrow into cakes of mash,
crushed and ground down
until only a powder remains, so fine,
as soft as a spider's caress,
as light as the breath of a child at sleep,
to be carried aloft in the rising heat
to meet the white of morning
—and all we can do
in that instant, leaning into the brace
of the wind, is surrender a cry.

IN THE COFFIN

Blood turns
to sludge
rusting veins.
Lungs collapse
the chest sinks.
Eyes now
a dull sheen
submerge
into sockets.
Thighs sag
then shrivel.
The mouth
exhales
as if forever.

But nails
keep growing.
The chin
sprouts stubble
flecks of light.
Teeth protrude
the tongue
coarsens.
Sour food
rots in the gut
bloating.
Excrement
leaks out as if
in protest.

WITHOUT END

"White clouds drift without end."
—Wang Wei, "Farewell"

The jade rabbit hides its elixir
        on the far side of the moon.
There is only night that is not night.

Eight immortals make up stories to laugh and cry,
        then shrug their shoulders.
There is only silence that is not silence.

In the temple venerable ancestors
        take our ghost money, and slip away.
There is only emptiness that is not emptiness.

Monks dance in circles, around and around,
        their chanting hoarse, gravelly.
There is only stillness that is not stillness.

A hermit journeys to the southern mountains,
        and gets lost in a maze of caves.
There is only an end that is not an end.

THE MURDER

"This was different from the death of people
in war, with weapons in their hands, the
deaths of people who had left behind their
houses, families, fields, songs, traditions
and stories. This was the murder of a great
and ancient professional experience, passed
from one generation to another in thousands
of families of craftsmen and members of the
intelligentsia."
                    —Vasily Grossman, *A Writer at War*

The barrel maker is dead
    caught in a mortar barrage
    unable to know which way to run.
The gaunt herbalist is dead
    wounded by a stray bullet
    his life then slowly bleeding away.
The ladies' tailor is dead
    his shop set on fire
    bolts of fabric ablaze all around him.
The bald nun is dead
    drowned trying to escape upstream
    when her overcrowded boat capsized.
The cobbler is dead
    killed while at work on the sidewalk
    shrapnel splattering flesh onto his shoes.
The photographer is dead
    shot in the face when he tried to stop
    the looting in his studio.
The stout policeman is dead
    slain by a machine gun burst
    when his barracks launched a counterattack.

Two spinster sisters are dead
    bayoneted on the floor of their home
    after being gang-raped.
The stonemason and his apprentices are dead
    buried alive in a large trench
    they and others had to dig.
The tall amah is dead
    poisoned by stolen opium she swallowed whole
    her choice of suicide over humiliation.
The waitresses are dead
    ripped apart by a grenade
    thrown through the door of their tea house.
The lantern maker's baby is dead
    her head bashed against a wall
    her parents speechless, unable to cry.
The newspaperman is dead
    tortured before being strangled
    for printing broadsheets urging resistance.
The burly fishmonger is dead
    his head split open by a sword
    to test how sharp the blade was.
The pregnant teacher is dead
    blown up by a land mine
    as she scoured alleyways for food.
The sign painter is dead
    pummeled into a coma,
    then lingering for days, defiant to the end.
The rice merchant is dead
    hit by a truck
    begrudging his hard life, his last thought.
The noodle shop owner is dead
    struck mute, unable to work,
    then refusing to eat.

The itinerant mender of pots is dead
    stabbed with his own pliers
    in front of his son who swore revenge.
The blind singer is dead
    chased down by dogs
    after she had been given a head start.
The tai chi master is dead
    starved in his cellar
    too shell-shocked to come out.
The young stevedore is dead
    beheaded on a wharf
    red-faced, full of tears, begging for mercy.
The street barber is dead
    thrown into the river
    along with his washstand, razors and mirror.
The petite mother and son are dead
    fallen from a second story window
    from which they had jumped or were pushed.
The fortune teller is dead
    his heart stopped when he heard
    that all of his children were dead.

SHE WILL NEVER

She will never chant nursery rhymes to her younger brothers,
    prepare hot water for the family tea shop,
    or play the hen guarding chicks with neighbor girls.

She will never help clean out her father's pigeon coops,
    join in the folk dances in the park at night,
    or embroider the apron for her dowry.

She will never catch the eye of the barrel-chested cobbler,
    see a mother's tears when she leaves home,
    or kneel to receive red envelopes from her new family.

She will never learn to steam her husband's favorite carp,
    mend his overcoat and attend to his bed,
    or answer him back and get away with it.

She will never scream during the birth of her daughter,
    teach her to bargain for vegetables at the market,
    or praise the straight edges of her weavings.

She will never mourn at her father-in-law's funeral,
    count the cash her husband brings back home each day,
    or pay from her own purse for her sons to learn to read.

She will never comb her hair lost in reverie,
    offer thanks to the Goddess of Mercy for their blessings,
    or climb the city ramparts to view the purple mountains.

She will never fear the bombs being dropped on our streets,
    hide as the demon soldiers march through the plaza,
    or wail as they bash her child's head against the wall.

As I have.

A SOLDIER RETURNS

> "I came to what had been our
> house and stood outside."
> —Claudia Emerson, "Aftermath"

I imagine the old lane, littered with rubble,
the gate to our courtyard torn down for firewood,
the plum trees shorn of leaves,
the walls of the houses inside still standing
but with their roofs caved in,
windows broken, front steps weathered and rotting,
suggesting that neighbors have escaped or are dead.

There is a small child working her way
up a mound of bricks near the well;
she must be my daughter, wide-eyed and squealing,
now able to run about with the chickens
as fast as her stout legs can carry her,
her braided pigtails trailing,
like butterflies fluttering this way and that.

My mother, head covered by her wide-brimmed hat,
squats in her garden, eyebrows knitted,
intent on plucking weeds from among the chives.
She is lost in her humming
—a village song that young wives,
their bellies pregnant, their hearts full of hope,
would chant at harvest time.

I also hear the familiar clacking of the loom
from just inside the shadows of the doorway,
its harnesses moving up and down,
a steady tattoo, as if in meditation,
to steel against any fear or sorrow,

the daily skirmishes beyond these broken walls,
even as death's hush grows ever closer.

Her senses alert, the weaver gets up
and steps out onto the threshold.
She is thinner than ever, chopstick-erect,
wearing the same clothes she wore the day I left.
Out of curiosity she peers about,
her eyes still adjusting to the light,
one bare foot rubbing the ankle of the other.

From her sad smile I know she has not remarried.
All they have now are each other,
two widows and a carefree girl.
In unison, they raise their eyes
attracted by the honking of wild geese,
in formation, flying south,
ragged lines across a sun-drenched sky.

THIS PHOTOGRAPH

"So many things recede and
fade like the colors and designs on stamps:
a nearly weightless letter, its sender."
—Leslie C. Chang, "Aerogramme"

Grandmother is seated,
leaning forward,
because by then
she was hunchbacked.
For this pose
she has removed
her spectacles
and squints intently,
mouth opened,
as if asking a question.
Behind her,
my mother stands
tall and erect,
her hands resting
on the high back
of the chair.
Her hair is cut short,
styled with bangs
covering her forehead.
In her dark, sleek dress
she looks on proudly,
as usual,
like a queen.
Reed-thin, I stand
in front of my grandmother
in my Western skirt
that flares out

from the waist.
My back is snuggled
against her knees.
Two long pigtails
fall to my shoulders;
I am playing
with one of them
with my hands,
fingernails neatly trimmed.
My front teeth
are exposed,
my eyes crinkle
—a foolish melon
of a grin.

This is the image
that we see
in this photograph,
but it is not the one
that I have
when I think of it now.
In my memories
of that day long ago,
I recall instead
the one who is not there,
the one whom
we were then watching,
our photographer,
hunched over,
peering down
into his camera box,
constantly fiddling
with the lens,
checking his light meter

and making sure
we were all
in a straight line.
He was our son,
our husband, our father
—always wearing
khaki pants,
shiny leather shoes,
and a pressed linen shirt.
His voice was
low and soft,
gently coaxing
each of us
to keep still,
be patient,
and to humor him,
for posterity's sake.

When we found his body
on the street
in front of our home,
this photograph
was in his billfold.
It was the one
he treasured most.
It is the one
I now hold
closest to my heart.

ELDER SISTER AND YOUNGER SISTER

They were true sisters, although their families lived on opposite sides of town. The one who was called Elder Sister had been born a few months earlier and was the youngest child of her family of seven. They lived by the river, next to the ruins of an ancient fort. Elder Sister's father was an itinerant tutor who went to the homes of rich families to teach their small children the rudiments of reading and writing. As such he was often not at home, moving in a circuit, staying with one family for several days, and then with another, and then another—only returning to his own home every few weeks.

Elder Sister discovered Younger Sister fetching water at the central well. She noticed that there was a girl as short as she was, who also wore her hair in a single braided pigtail. Soon after, they were each other's constant companion, running about the back streets. The older girl was light skinned, with a long, lean face, large eyes and pointed nose, matching her serious nature, in contrast to her new friend whose complexion was dark and who had a round, chubby face and an impish smile. Nonetheless, both from the beginning intuited that theirs was a special relationship that would carry them through for the rest of their lives.

If the two could meet after chores, they were at Younger Sister's home. Elder Sister's family was so busy that they hardly ever knew or wondered where their child had gone. But Younger Sister's family, which included a much younger brother, was more than happy with this new visitor. Younger Sister's father was a gatherer of medicinal herbs and taught the two of them which herbs to mix together for his remedies for various common ailments.

Some days Elder Sister would bring a drawing that she had made, using leftover rice paper her father brought home. He actually taught her only the mechanics: washing the brush thoroughly, lightly grinding down the hard inkstick into the thin pool of water that had been poured sparingly onto the inkslab, and then holding the brush vertically, keeping her forearm horizontal, as parallel to the table as she could control. Capturing an image of a flower in the bud, or a fat fish, or a many-sided rock dancing in the play of lights and shadows—this was a talent that Elder Sister developed on her own. Her father took note of her achievements, but not being very ambitious for any of his daughters, he never encouraged anything more.

Often the two girls would explore the bamboo grove nearby, reveling in the dappled morning light. Neighbor boys returning from the rice paddies with their catch of frogs would sometimes see them cuddling together, lying on a bed of moss at the edge of a clearing. The boys might call out, but the girls would ignore them, or just wave and go back to whispering with each other their gossips of the day.

As the girls grew older, however, Elder Sister's family became more concerned. Rumors circulated that the two had not outgrown their mutual infatuation; they were now unhealthily inseparable. Elder Sister's mother especially decided that this daughter should finally be matched with a boy, and without much discussion even with her husband she made arrangements for her daughter to be wed. When Elder Sister heard the news she let out a shout and quickly ran over to her friend's home. The two were distraught for days, and it seemed powerless for them to fight the inevitable. Younger Sister's mother tried to convince them of how happy each would eventually be raising their own families, but the girls would have none of it. They were headstrong and too single-minded to heed others' reasoning. They had different plans and schemed in secret to run away to the city together.

Indeed, on one summer day while the families were distracted, preparing for the festival of the cowherd and the weaving maiden, the two friends set out. Before anyone really was aware of it, they were halfway to their destination. Search parties were sent out into the bamboo grove and along the river, but no one ever thought they would have even dared to strike out for the city. But they did.

∾

Elder Sister and Younger Sister realized that their love for each other
was something unique, but that consequently others would nonethe-
less disapprove. They were never ones to do anyone any harm. They
were in love and believed that the happiness they shared could also be
shared with those around them, akin to honey in a jar overflowing,
sweetening its surroundings. Yes, the two were still young and felt
impervious to the woes of the world. But their naivete was tempered
knowing that some looked upon their relationship with intolerance
(it was in their nature to be circumspect, so they never returned the
scorn). In the city, they started telling those they encountered that
they were indeed sisters. They did not really look alike; after a spurt,
Elder Sister had grown much taller, with a large bosom, taking after
her mother. But no one ever thought otherwise. They were so close
to each other, so sensitive to each other's feelings; where there were
differences in interests and behavior each appeared to complement the
other.

Somehow they also knew that they were destined to suffer for this
daring. Nevertheless, they were willing to make such a sacrifice for
what they understood—without ever articulating it—was the extraor-
dinariness of their lives together.

At first they lived on the streets. This was not so unusual for the coun-
try was poor, and many other inhabitants survived from day to day
in this way. Luckily, they soon discovered an orphanage run by nuns
who took them in. The two girls' abilities were readily apparent, and
they became favorites who were given supervision over other children.
They seemed so assured and generous with their love. In return the
orphanage nurtured the sisters. Elder Sister's natural gifts in paint-
ing were refined, especially under the guidance of the head abbess.
Younger Sister shared her knowledge of all the herbs that she learned

210

from her father. An apprenticeship in an herb shop was found, with her earnings given over to the temple.

Although they were always grateful for their years at the orphanage, as they grew older the sisters were nonetheless uncomfortable with the expectation that they would stay there indefinitely. The nuns assumed they would someday enter their order, which Younger Sister was especially resistant in doing. Working outside in the herb stop, she was more exposed to the varieties of living experiences, and after some discussion the sisters agreed to leave the orphanage to make their way on their own.

What was left unsaid was, if they found a place where they could be alone for the first time, they could fully live just for themselves without always looking over their shoulders, without others' prying eyes. It was this attraction that hastened their leaving. With the nuns' kind assistance they moved into a tiny room which only allowed for a bunk bed, and a small table and chair against a narrow window. They slept on the bottom bed; their few belongings they kept above them. More importantly, there were four walls offering them the privacy to discover even more their love for each other. They shared their daily rituals, they shared their dreams. They confessed secret passions and their most shameful deeds. In the summers the room turned into a furnace. Naked, their skins glistened from their copious sweating. They did not mind. It was as if they were drifting on the surface of a pond in the noonday heat, existing only for the present moment, these two souls intertwined. It was the most rapturous time of their lives.

Younger Sister continued to work at the herb shop, and the owner, an older widower with no children, gradually shared with her his knowledge of the business. She was reserved but took the time to listen to customers. They liked the way she was genuinely concerned for their well-being. Often direct, she revealed a wry humor to those who got to know her more; a few began stopping by just to say hello.

Elder Sister stayed at home, doing all the housekeeping and cooking. Usually after her midday snack when the afternoon light entered their room she would practice her painting, her one indulgence. She could still recall much of the landscape of the town they had come from, and these visions gave her a grounding; she felt a modest sense of accomplishment. Her neighbors in the building all marveled at her work; they suggested she find a way to sell her paintings so that the sisters would no longer need to live so impoverished a life. But it was not something Elder Sister ever considered.

By the time the war came a few years passed. Like many others the sisters did not know whether to stay or try to leave. In the end they believed that they had already been blessed by their lives in the city and remained where they were. Unfortunately, after the city was stormed and surrendered, the invaders ran amok, killing indiscriminately, looting and raping. The sisters stayed in their room, hoping to wait out the demon soldiers' furies, although it meant that they would have to ration further the little foodstuffs they had stockpiled away. Even the great locusts come and go.

After several weeks, neighbors who had also remained began to venture out of the building. It was believed that those who were poor and led simple lives could go back to what they had been doing before the demons had arrived. Younger Sister helped re-open the herb shop with the owner, hoping that business would resume. But three of the occupiers one day entered the shop looking for money, and when they could not find any they took out their anger by locking the two inside the shop and then setting the premises on fire. Both bodies were found later, charred beyond recognition. Even Elder Sister could not distinguish which corpse was her sister, and which was not.

~

From then on Elder Sister shrouded herself in mourning. Day and night she had nothing to hold on to, no way to share her grief. She did not eat, she did not speak. She took to wearing her hair long. A keening filled her ears, and she was deaf to all else. Her worried neighbors asked the nuns at the temple if they would care for her. But though the abbess sent word for her to return, Elder Sister steadfastly refused, wishing to remain in her room, to cling to whatever remnants of her life with her sister were left.

The nuns were again helpful in finding Elder Sister a place to work; this provided enough cash for her to sustain her frugal life. She was naturally good with her hands and assisted the owner of a store which made baskets and even chairs and tables out of wicker. It was, she conceded, better than being cooped up in her room by herself. Her neighbors and the others at work were respectful of her but also left her alone out of consideration for her recluse ways.

The war ended shortly thereafter. Everyone looked forward to opening up new chapters in their lives. It would be hard work as the country had been devastated, but after so many dark years people were willing to hope for something more. The owner of her store suggested that even Elder Sister should move on. (In fact, he knew of a few men who had lost their wives during the war and offered to make introductions.) Elder Sister was not sure though. She had managed to get by on her own for so long now. She knew that she needed to seize each day as it came. But she still felt within her, in her heart, an emptiness which she believed would never be filled again. She bore it like a heavy weight anchoring her to her room.

One day, a huge typhoon swept the city. No one dared to go outdoors. Strong winds entered Elder Sister's room through the gaps in the window frames, swirling about in the confines of her tiny space, like trapped bats, upending many of her possessions. She sat still, hugging her knees in the corner of her bed, and listened carefully to each thunderclap as it lashed out like a giant whip. Night turned to day for brief electrical moments, nature's displays of raw power against which all human life will appear puny.

After the storm subsided, after sunlight reappeared in the sky, Elder Sister set about cleaning up her room. There was a dampness everywhere. There was a fine layer of grit upon everything. She started with her top bunk, and then her bed and her small table and the windows. She mopped down the walls and picked up everything that lay on the floor, carefully wiping each item before placing it on her top bunk. Under her bed, against a wall, she found the cardboard box filled with her painting implements—the inkslab, inksticks, her brushes, and sheets of rice paper. After Younger Sister had died, she had without regret put aside her artwork. The daily struggle was enough, she told herself, though that was just an excuse not to remind herself of their former contentment.

She was sitting at the table as she inspected the contents of the box for any damage. Without thinking she picked up one of the brushes and held it as if focusing her whole body within her hand's grasp—just the way her father had first showed her. She moved her arm as if painting a few strokes, tentatively, a field mouse learning to walk again after a deep winter's sleep.

In an instant Elder Sister recalled the bamboo grove which she had painted so many times before. It was the spot where she and her sister had first escaped to, every chance they could. It was where they first confided with each other and where they first kissed. It was where, full of joy, they exchanged vows never to leave each other no matter what. She was taken aback by these memories; she thought she should look upon them fondly, but on this day there was only pain.

Over the years, on occasion, she had rationalized that their relationship had been so intense as to more than make up for its brevity. In the marriages of their parents, for instance, their mutual affections had been even more fleeting. She should be satisfied that Younger Sister had given her enough love for several more lifetimes to come. But she knew deep down that this was a lie. The sisters had been cheated. She was right to begrudge her present existence.

Elder Sister acknowledged there were others who had been damaged during this war. She was not so very special, and many had endured so much more suffering than she. And she was alive too, though at times she thought she should have not been spared. But to survive had its own burdens. The wondrous past with Younger Sister was irredeemable, and the hard future without her was unbearable. This was the essence of Elder Sister's sorrow. Nonetheless, that fate had betrayed them did not mean then that she would betray Younger Sister. It was this insight that saved her, and staying true to it was the only choice, humble as it was, that she felt she could embrace.

The direct afternoon sun again shone through her window breaking her reverie. She now noticed that she had been weeping, though for how long she was not sure. Her clothes and the table were moist. The inkslab which had been removed from the box also contained more of her tears. It seemed as if she could make enough ink to paint a solitary twig of bamboo. In her mind's eye, it would be thin and straight, hollow within, and yet utterly unbreakable.

EPILOGUE

"…of who was still living
and who had died and why."

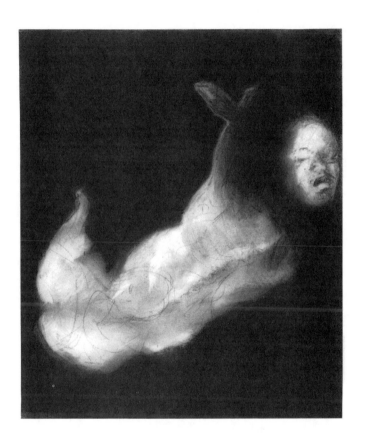

A YOUNG GIRL IN A CHEONGSAM

She is sitting with her cheongsam
pulled up around her waist.
She grimaces, eyes downcast,
her face is near black.
But her hands and legs
in this photograph
appear bleached out.
Her cunt in the shadows of her crotch
is a dark blur
spread open by her fingers,
her nails neatly trimmed
glinting in the sunlight.
The outline of her inner lips stands out
—two parts of an inverted Y—
with the ridge of her clitoris
protruding like a promontory
overlooking a ravished valley.

Her cheongsam is the kind
that so many other young girls
also wore in those old days in China:
the high collar, side opening,
side slits at the hem.
It is the kind of dress
which my mother wore
when she was also young,
a dress slightly padded
and with long sleeves for the winter,
a kind of dress
that fills the photograph album
that my mother brought with her
when she came to Hawaii to be married

before the war,
before the Japanese invaded.

There is an apocryphal story
that my mother at one time
interrupted her studies
to visit relatives in Nanjing
because of fighting in Shanghai.
I do not know
whether it was the Japanese then,
more likely the warlords instead.
There are still photographs
of her stay in her album:
younger cousins it seems
crowded about her.
All the girls wear cheongsam,
some brighter than others,
some more distinctly patterned.
Their faces are smiling, even glowing.
How many were there ten years later?
How many survived The Rape?

My mother died before I was aware
of all of the horrors in the world.
I knew there had been a war,
I knew she had been lucky to escape it.
But those who were raped
and those who were killed
like this young girl spread out before me,
I would never have dared to contemplate.

I suspect my mother did.
I think she would have found out,
word of mouth from refugees
or at least after the war

even if her letters were returned,
if others in Shanghai had written her,
if others in Hong Kong
when we visited my grandfather in 1952
had whispered of its immensity,
of who was still living
and who had died and why.

This young girl is not one of our relatives
though she could have been
—I imagine, a younger aunt perhaps,
someone that I might meet today
on the street bent over
buying vegetables at the Open Market,
a small wizened tiger of a woman
still wearing a cheongsam
as my mother did
up to the time she died.

My mother had she stayed
would likely have met
the same indiscriminate fate.
And when I look at the photograph
there is a special sorrow.
I think of her
sitting in this young girl's place
baring that which gave me birth,
a witness so rude and raw
as to confirm
my blood existence as mere whim.

NOTES

Too often history is written by those who survive, those who won (the pen then works in service to the sword). The victims of war, especially those who did not survive, seldom have their experiences told. No one knows what happened to them, too often no one cares. Their lives, their sufferings must be recounted to provide a true memorial. It is up to creative writers to imagine the stories of those who have been forgotten, whose existence may have been deliberately erased. These are stories which are perforce fiction, not autobiography, not memoir, yet nonetheless can ring true. In doing so, bearing witness also provides some small measure of revenge against their victors (in this case the pen is taken up in opposition to the sword).

The Nanjing Massacre—when Japan invaded China in 1937, ultimately capturing its capital and in six weeks wreaking havoc on its surrendering military defenders and civilian inhabitants alike—poses additional ironies. China as a part of the Allied cause eventually prevailed in its war of resistance against Japan. Nevertheless, some Japanese, in their writing of this history in their school textbooks 75 years afterwards, continue to deny, or at least minimize, the atrocities. It was her outrage over this denial which moved me when I read Iris Chang's *The Rape of Nanking* (New York: Basic Books, 1997). Subsequently, I found enough other books on the subject to believe that a massacre did indeed occur. It was this source material which has become the basis for my narrative poems, now totaling these 100-odd creative pieces, written over the past 15 years.

Admittedly, I did not set out to write a book of poems. Contrary to what novelists may do, I did not consciously embark on a long term project, to write this full length collection from beginning to end, as the poems are now ordered. Instead, after Chang, I discovered the following books which I consider an essential bibliography:

James Yin and Shi Young, *The Rape of Nanking: An Undeniable History in Photographs* (Chicago: Innovative Publishing Group, 1996);

Honda Katsuichi, *The Nanjing Massacre* (Armonk: M. E. Sharpe, 1999);

The Good Man of Nanking: The Diaries of John Rabe (New York: Knopf, 1998); and

Hua-ling Hu and Zhang Lian-hong, eds., *The Undaunted Women of Nanking, The Wartime Diaries of Minnie Vautrin and Tsen Shui-fang* (Carbondale: Southern Illinois University Press, 2010).

These four books described the massacre on a human scale, the first through surviving photographs, the second through narratives based on interviews of victims or diaries or testimonies of perpetrators, and the last two through diaries of those who tried to provide sanctuary for the civilians. For me, they offered unique windows on how to comprehend this historical event, as a collection of individual events that happened to individual people.

Initially what piqued my interest was to see if I could recreate what I saw and what I read in poetic form, and my first attempts were more closely based on specific recorded events. I thought the handful of poems I came up with might become a separate section of my next volume of poetry. However, more books on this historical event started appearing on local bookstore shelves. Some dealt with the soldiers, others the comfort women, and still others the civilians struggling to survive. So I appropriated, opportunistically, what I was reading at the time, and these poems were more loosely inspired by my readings (i.e., not strictly based on them). This was especially true if there was a unique anecdote that was only two or three sentences long; I decided to flesh out the historical record, through my fiction, to bring it more vividly to life.

Additionally, I was reading other books on other wars—though primarily on World War II in other theatres. I also have tried to keep up with contemporary American poetry. From these readings, there were a few situations which I decided to transpose to this Nanjing Massacre period. Lastly, I began to write poems which are essentially invented by me. Therefore, for many of these poems I cannot provide a specific footnote to cite that such and such an event did actually occur.

In my mind, the stories being told are still what James Wood has called "the plausibly hypothetical…what Aristotle claimed was the difference between the historian and the poet: the former describes what happened, and the latter what might happen." (in "Invitation to a Beheading," *The New Yorker*, May 7, 2012). I sincerely hope that collectively these poems still serve as a cumulative testament to the qualitative and quantitative immensity of this massacre.

I would like to provide some insight as to how I came to write individual poems, as follows:

PART ONE

"The Wall" was inspired by a reading of the engineering achievements of the Ming Dynasty's first emperor, Zhu Yuanzhang, in Michael E. Haskew, Christer Jorgensen, Chris McNab, Eric Niderost and Rob S. Rice, *Fighting Techniques of the Oriental World* (New York: Thomas Dunne Books, 2008). In 2009 I was able to visit a portion of the wall still standing, Zhonghua Gate; even now this remnant is an imposing structure.

"Preferential Certificate" is a found poem, a translation of a flyer found in Yin and Shi.

"Our Scorched Earth Policy" was inspired by the diary entry of Wang Mengsong for May 15, 1941, when he fled from his village in Zhejiang Province, in R. Keith Schoppa, *In a Sea of Bitterness* (Cambridge: Harvard University Press, 2011). I was especially taken by Schoppa's wry observation that the Wang family took "*a none-too subtle culinary scorched-earth approach.*"

"The Hand Cart" was inspired by a photograph found in Jack Birns, *Assignment Shanghai* (Berkeley: University of California Press, 2003). It is of a refugee family fleeing Shanghai during the Chinese civil war in April, 1949, and I transposed this image to Nanjing in 1937.

"Fleeing" was inspired by reading about Parisians fleeing the German army at the beginning of World War II, in Hanna Diamond, *Fleeing Hitler, France 1940* (Oxford: Oxford University Press, 2007).

"The Peach Boys" was inspired by reading about the use of this famous Japanese folktale as propaganda to justify the invasion of China, in two books by John Dower, *War without Mercy* (New York: Pantheon, 1986), and *Embracing Defeat* (New York: Norton, 1999). After I wrote this poem, I read Robert Tierney, *Tropics of Savagery* (Berkeley: University of California Press, 2010), which offers the same observation for Japan's colonization of the South Seas.

"The Night Before" was inspired by anecdotes of Japanese soldiers preparing for battle, in Kazuo Tamayama and John Nunneley, *Tales by Japanese Soldiers* (London: Cassell, 2000).

"I Hold My Breath" was inspired by an anecdote related by Suhara Seiichi, in Frank Gibney, *Senso* (Armonk: M. E. Sharpe, 1995). My wording is essentially Suhara's; I could not come up with a better description of his experience.

In "Haiku" the second poem was inspired by an anecdote in Vasily Grossman, *A Writer at War* (New York: Vintage, 2007).

"In a Deserted Camp" was inspired by an anecdote in Craig Collie and Hajime Marutani, *The Path of Infinite Sorrow* (Crow's Nest: Allen & Unwin, 2009), describing the experiences of Japanese soldiers on the Kokoda Trail; I then transposed it to this war.

"Inside Zhongshan Gate" was inspired by an anecdote related by Private Itamoto Shiro, in Honda.

"A Real Soldier" was inspired by an anecdote in E. B. Sledge, *With the Old Breed: At Peleliu and Okinawa* (New York: Ballantine, 1981). However, I have made my poem even more disgusting.

The situation described in "The Near Dead" was inspired by "The Chore," a poem by Frannie Lindsay.

"I Am Not Dead" was inspired by an observation found in John Rabe's diary entry for January 22, 1938. I felt that somehow I needed to give this one "poor devil" a voice.

"A Kimono" was inspired by my viewing of a kimono in an exhibit at the Honolulu Academy of Arts in 2007, and then reading its exhibition catalog, Jacqueline M. Atkins, *Wearing Propaganda: Textiles on the Home Front in Japan, Britain, and the United States, 1931-1945* (New Haven: Yale University Press, 2005).

PART TWO

"At the Foot of Mufu Mountain" was inspired by field diaries of soldiers of the Morozumi Unit, in Honda.

"The Red Circle" was inspired by an anecdote related by Kawano Masato, in Gibney.

"New Recruits" was inspired by photographs in Yin and Shi, and elsewhere.

"Thrown into the Earth" was inspired by photographs in Yin and Shi, and elsewhere.

"The Beheader" was inspired by statements made by First Lieutenant Uno Shintaro in Honda, and elsewhere.

"A Perversion" was inspired by a pair of photographs in Yin and Shi. They appear to have been taken nearly simultaneously, and I have imagined, in this poem, that such timing was not mere coincidence.

"My Reward" was inspired by an anecdote in Robert Leckie, *Helmet for My Pillow* (New York: Bantam, 1957), describing his experiences as a Marine in the Pacific in World War II; I then transposed it to this war.

"The Boots" was inspired by an anecdote in Catherine Merridale, *Ivan's War* (New York: Picador, 2006), describing the experiences of ordinary Russian soldiers during World War II; I then transposed it to this war.

"Pragmatic" and "Capricious" were written at the same time. The events described are based on specific anecdotes found in R. J. Rummell, *China's Bloody Century* (New Brunswick: Transaction Publishers, 1991); Yin and Shi; Haruko Taya Cook and Theodore F. Cook, *Japan at War* (New York: Norton, 1992); Honda; diary entries of John G. Magee and of Albert N. Steward, in Zhang Kaiyuan, ed., *Eyewitnesses to Massacre* (Armonk: M. E. Sharpe, 2001); and Xu Zhigeng, *Lest We Forget: Nanjing Massacre, 1937* (Beijing: Chinese Literature Press, 1995). After reading testimony by witnesses before the Tokyo War Crimes Trial, Rummell in addition observed that while today we might find their actions shocking the Japanese themselves may have had "practical" reasons for what they did. So I tried to find those atrocities which might be explained in such a way, and I compiled them in the first poem. However, there were still many others that to me were more a result of cruel whim; these I felt belonged in a second poem.

"The Resistance" was inspired by descriptions of Chinese resisters who remained in Nanjing after the fall of the city, in Xu.

"The Sniper" was inspired by an observation in "Storm over the Pacific", an article by Dennis Showalter, in Daniel Marston, ed., *The Pacific War Companion* (Oxford: Osprey Publishing, 2005).

"In the Darkroom" was inspired by an article, with photographs, entitled "Killing for Fun!" in *Look* (November 22, 1938). This article was mentioned in Chang, and elsewhere. In 2009 I went to the New York City Public Library to obtain a microfilm copy of the original publication. I then tried to imagine how the Chinese photography studio workers felt when they decided to smuggle out the extra prints.

"Army Doctors" describes a period after the initial Nanjing Massacre. It was inspired by statements made by Yuasa Ken, a military doctor, in Cook and Cook; I wrote from his point of view.

"Unit 1644" describes a period after the initial Nanjing Massacre. It was inspired by a chapter in Simon Winchester, *The River at the Center of the World* (New York: Henry Holt, 1996). This unit was affiliated with the infamous Unit 731, and also conducted biological and chemical warfare experiments on humans. I gathered more information on this unit in Daniel Barenblatt, *A Plague on Humanity* (New York: HarperCollins, 2004); Hal Gold, *Unit 731 Testimony* (Boston: Tuttle, 1966); and Sheldon Harris, *Factories of Death* (London: Routledge, 1994).

"Double Crimes" was written because I noticed in my readings that many crimes suffered by the Chinese soldiers who surrendered as well as by the noncombatant civilians also ended with the ultimate crime of murder. During the Nanjing Massacre period I think it was because of the invaders' concerns to remove evidence of the first crimes.

PART THREE

"Nanjing, December, 1937" was the first poem written in this series, a compilation of the more egregious atrocities which I discovered in reading Chang in 1997.

"The Nanking Safety Zone" refers to a sanctuary established for civilians. It soon became crowded, and my poem imagines the plight of a mother who arrived late to one of the refugee areas.

"We Watch" is based on Private Azuma Shiro's diary entry for April 7, 1938, in *The Diary of Azuma Shiro* (Nanjing: Phoenix Publishing, 2006).

"Golden Lotuses" is based on a discovery near the Little Jinlian Bridge confirmed by a Japanese prisoner of war, as reported in Honda. I did additional research on bound feet and their special shoes in Beverly Jackson, *Splendid Slippers* (Berkeley: Ten Speed Press, 1997).

"Kanji" refers to the Chinese characters used in written Japanese. This poem was inspired by my reading of how language can reveal cultural values of a society, in Kittredge Cherry, *Womansword* (Tokyo: Kodansha, 1987).

"Just Punishment" was inspired by an anecdote in Xu.

"An Autopsy at the Moment of Death" is a wholly invented poem. However, its structure is copied from a poem entitled "On the Death of a New Born Child" by Mei Yaochen, a Song Dynasty poet.

"In this Pose" was based on a photograph in Yin and Shi.

"They Were Markers" was inspired by a certain police study on the further desecration of women who were raped and then murdered, in Susan Brownmiller, *Against Our Will* (New York: Fawcett, 1975). The euphemism used then was "extravagant defilements." I found mention of this peculiar practice by Japanese soldiers not only in Brownmiller, but also in Honda, Chang, M. J. Thurman and Christine A. Sherman, *War Crimes: Japan's World War II Atrocities* (Paducah: Turner, 2001), and Yin and Shi.

"A Moment of the Truest Horror" was actually written prior to this series, but I decided it could still fit in this collection. Incidents such as the one described have been confirmed by the testimony of a former Staff Sergeant T, in Honda.

"On the Day before Christmas" is based on a well-known standoff between missionaries who were in charge of the sanctuary for women and children at Jinling College and Japanese authorities who needed women to serve in their brothel. It was recorded in the diary entries of Minnie Vautrin and Tsen Shui-fang for December 24, 1937, both in Hu and Zhang. However, not as well-known is John Rabe's diary entry for two days later, recounting (I believe secondhand) how this confrontation was actually resolved. So even among diary entries there may be variations on what actually occurred. I have used Rabe's version for the ending to my poem. Lastly, as a point of clarification, the Red Swastika Society has nothing to do with Nazi Germany, and instead refers to a traditional Chinese relief organization which undertook to bury corpses during the Nanjing Massacre.

"The Lesson" was inspired by an anecdote in Minnie Vautrin's diary entry for December 17, 1937, in Hu and Zhang. I have however written my poem from the point of view of one of the Japanese soldiers.

"Our Mission" was inspired by my visit to John Rabe's home in Nanjing in 2009. I was especially struck by how relatively low the walls were (about 7 feet) surrounding his property. I recalled reading of complaints by Rabe and other missionaries about Japanese soldiers scaling their walls to kidnap women who were living within their compounds. I wrote this poem imagining such a mission from the point of view of one of the soldiers.

"White Tiger" was inspired by the experience of a Dutch comfort woman in Indonesia, Jan Ruff-O'Herne, in her memoir *50 Years of Silence* (North

Sydney: William Heinemann, 1994). I was especially intrigued by her unusual act of defiance. This and the next several poems about comfort women actually describe a period after the initial Nanjing Massacre; it is related, however, as the Japanese authorities decided to curb the opportunistic rapes by establishing comfort stations later on.

"The Belt" was inspired by a striking drawing made by Maria Rosa Henson, a Filipino comfort woman, in her memoir *Comfort Woman* (Lanham: Rowman & Littlefield, 1999).

"Naked" was inspired by a photograph I saw when I visited the Nanjing Massacre Memorial Hall in 2009. It was of a comfort woman, standing naked and looking into the camera. In 2003 Pak Yongsim of Korea returned to Nanjing to identify herself as the woman, then in her early 20s, in the photograph; she also visited the building, still standing, which served as her comfort station. I wrote this poem in her voice, as if at the very moment of this photograph.

"The Chair" was based on a photograph taken by Aso Tetsuo, in his memoir *From Shanghai to Shanghai* (Norwalk: East Bridge, 2004). He served as a doctor in several comfort stations in China.

"Best Attack" was based on a photograph taken by Aso Tetsuo, in Aso.

"Living-Dead" was inspired by my reading of the treatment of comfort women in Mark Driscoll, *Absolute Erotic, Absolute Grotesque: The Living, Dead, and Undead in Japan's Imperialism, 1895 – 1945* (Durham: Duke University Press, 2010).

"Rapes" was written because I noticed that many of the reported rapes of the Nanjing Massacre resulted in the murder of the victim as well, in Ian Buruma, *The Wages of Guilt* (London: Phoenix, 1994), in Honda, and elsewhere. I then tried to compare what happened in Nanjing with similar wartime rapes in Berlin, in Anonymous, *A Woman in Berlin* (New York: Metropolitan, 2000); in the Congo, in Brownmiller; in Bosnia, in Roy Guttman and David Rieff, eds., *Crimes of War* (New York: Norton, 1999); and in Rwanda, in Jean Hatzfeld, *Machete Season* (New York: Farrar, Straus and Giroux, 2003).

"After Okichi" is based on an event described in the two books by Dower.

PART FOUR

"Plum Blossoms" was inspired by my viewing of a painting by Liu Shiru, entitled "Plum in Snow" at the Metropolitan Museum, New York City, in 2009, and then learning more about the symbolism of plums in Chinese culture.

"How I Am to End" was inspired by memoirs of civilians who had been kidnapped to serve as porters, in Shoppa.

"They" was inspired by comments on *chankoro* ("chinks") made by Private Iwao Ajiro, in Max Hastings, *Retribution* (New York: Vintage, 2009).

"This Reasoning," "Our Actress," and "What the Interpreter Saw" were inspired by Tsen Shui-fang's diary entries for December 19, 1937, December 29, 1937, and January 2, 1938, respectively, in Hu and Zhang. Tsen in her diary appears to have been more skeptical and displaying a greater sense of outrage than her Jinling College colleague, Minnie Vautrin. For the first of these poems, I tried to recreate in a dramatic way the differences of opinion between Tsen and another missionary. For the second, I imagined a scene that might have taken place, to give life to Tsen's bare bones diary entry report of this heroic act. Then for the third, I wrote my poem from the point of view of a third party, the interpreter, who observes both Tsen and the visitors to her school.

"We Do Not Need to Ask" and "A Game We All Play" were inspired by the diary entries of both Minnie Vautrin and Tsen Shui-fang, for January 20, 1938, and for February 3 and 4, 1938, respectively, in Hu and Zhang. Reading their entries side by side offers a fuller picture of the events described. Tsen, probably because her Chinese was much better, was able to learn more about what was really happening. I wrote both of these poems from her point of view.

"A Pot of Rice Gruel" and "The Scavenger" were inspired by John Rabe's diary entries for January 25, 1938 and January 7, 1938, respectively. I doubt that Rabe himself witnessed these events; he likely recorded anecdotes he heard secondhand.

"A Soldier's Report" was inspired by anecdotes related by Ishida Yahachi and Kawakami Sada, both of whom fought in the Pacific in World War II, in Gibney; I then transposed them to this war.

"Hunger" imagines how three women tried to survive hiding out, without food. A book on American nurses interred by the Japanese in the Philippines, Elizabeth M. Norman, *We Band of Angels* (New York: Random House, 1999), provided me with specific details which I could transpose for this poem.

"Where We Left Our Family" was inspired by an anecdote related by Luo Daxing, then seven years old, in Honda. In many places, my wording is essentially Luo's; I could not come up with a better description of his experience.

"Unrighteous" and "As Usual" were inspired by two anecdotes found in a historical romance in *Record of Military Subjugation in the Yu Hills and the Sea*, recounting the 1645 Qing conquest of Changshu County, in Lynn A. Struve, Ed., *Voices from the Ming-Qing Cataclysm* (New Haven: Yale University Press, 1993). I transposed both situations to this war, one as a dramatic piece with three voices, and the other as a narrative poem.

The situation described in "The Chinese Violin" was inspired by "Keyboard," a poem by Robert Pinsky. The title refers to an *er hu*, a two-stringed instrument held vertically on one's lap and played with a bow; although somewhat misleading, I have translated it as a Chinese violin.

PART FIVE

"The Professional Mourners" was inspired by a chapter on this profession in modern day China in Liao Yiwu, *The Corpse Walker* (New York: Pantheon Books, 2008). So I imagined what such mourners would have done in Nanjing as this massacre unfolded.

"In the Coffin" is for Juliet.

"The Murder" was inspired by my reading of a passage in Grossman, about how war can destroy a whole civilization, one individual at a time.

The situation described in "A Soldier Returns" was inspired by "Aftermath," a poem by Claudia Emerson.

"Elder Sister and Younger Sister" is for Judy.

EPILOGUE

"A Young Girl in a Cheongsam" was based a photograph in Yin and Shi. Gayle K. Sato has written a paper, entitled "Witnessing Atrocity through Auto-biography: Wing Tek Lum's *The Nanjing Massacre: Poems*," which includes a close reading of this specific poem. To continue our dialogue, I in turn responded with a short essay, "Notes to Gayle Sato," further reflecting on this poem. Both pieces are being published in *Inter-Asia Cultural Studies* 13: 2 (June 2012), and may be found online at http://www.tandfonline.com/riac.

ACKNOWLEDGEMENTS

I must first acknowledge my debt to the late Iris Chang, whose book *The Rape of Nanking* raised my awareness of the Nanjing Massacre. I wish also to thank the many other historians who published additional books on the subject, especially those cited in my Notes, to present a fuller picture of this historical event.

I started writing these poems in 1997, and submitted my initial drafts to the Study Group affiliated with Bamboo Ridge Press. I have been blessed by the steadfastness of these fellow writers who month after month served as the first critics and supporters for each and every one of these poems.

Earlier versions of several of these poems have already been published in literary journals. I wish to express my appreciation to their editors for giving the following wider recognition:

Asian American Resource Workshop Newsletter: "A Moment of the Truest Horror."

Poetry: "Nanjing, December, 1937."

TriQuarterly: "A Young Girl in a Cheongsam," "Pragmatic," and "Capricious."

Amerasia Journal: "The Night before," "At the Foot of Mufu Mountain," "The Beheader," "Golden Lotuses," "Army Doctors," and "Unit 1644."

Zyzzyva: "Escaping the War."

Michigan Quarterly Review: "Hair."

Bamboo Ridge: "What I Learned from Your College Annual," "The Near Dead," "New Recruits," "Thrown into the Earth," "A Village Burial," "A Soldier Returns," and "The Murder."

Kaimana: "All Her Love Forever," "In the Coffin," and "Even Our Bones."

Asian American Literary Review: "The Nanking Safety Zone," "Inside Her Wooden Chest," "The Professional Mourners," "The Scavenger," and "The Rice."

After reaching a critical mass of poems, I started sharing them with fellow writers outside of my Study Group to give me a fresh look. And when this collection was nearing completion, I also asked a few historians to review my manuscript from their unique perspectives. The responses in all cases were encouraging, and gave me the confidence to finally publish these poems in book form. I must humbly thank the following: Jeffery Paul Chan, Ken Chen,

Edward Fitzgerald, Kimiko Hahn, Russell Leong, Shan Te-hsing, Cathy Song, Daniel W. Y. Kwok, Yuma Totani, and Daqing Yang. In addition, Ha Jin has served as a unique role model for me, since I knew that he was also writing on this event with his novel *Nanjing Requiem*. Lastly, I need to single out Gayle K. Sato, a literary critic, for special mention; although I prefer to say that my poems should speak for themselves, she has pushed me to become more articulate about what I have been trying to do in this series and why.

The Cooke Foundation committed funds, sight unseen, to help underwrite the publication of this collection. The Cades Foundation has for more than a decade supported the overall literary activities of Bamboo Ridge Press. In my role as its business manager, I am on a daily basis conscious of the financial precarity of little magazines. Accordingly, I am very grateful especially for these two financial angels, both in Hawaii, who have given this press the critical support necessary to make this book a reality.

Founding editors, Eric Chock and Darrell Lum, and managing editor, Joy Kobayashi-Cintrón, are my colleagues at this press. Notwithstanding this, they were tolerant enough to accept this manuscript for publication. They along with Marie Hara, Michael Little, Normie Salvador, Lanning Lee, and Rowen Tabusa then shepherded its production. I trust I need not mention my abiding aloha for all of them.

Several years ago Noe Tanigawa asked to read this series of poems. To my surprise she then proceeded to create three paintings and about 80 black and white vellum drawings inspired by individual poems. This became the wonderful "excavation table" she displayed as part of the "Degrees of Distinction" exhibit at the University of Hawaii in 2009. This past year, several drawings were also featured in *Bamboo Ridge* #98. I am grateful that she has allowed me to use even more of her work for the cover and interior art of this book.

Lastly, I am dedicating this book to my mother. Through her I do have a very slight, tenuous connection to Nanjing, just prior to the war. More so, I learned from her a kindness—this basic antidote to war—which has carried me through my life, and through the writing of these poems. Two other generations, my wife and my daughter, complete the trio of the most important women in my life. For these last two, I promise to dedicate future volumes of poetry. Until then, I can only offer my love.

Wing Tek Lum is a Honolulu businessman and poet. His first collection of poetry, *Expounding the Doubtful Points*, was published by Bamboo Ridge Press in 1987. With Makoto Ooka, Joseph Stanton, and Jean Yamasaki Toyama, he participated in a collaborative work of linked verse, which was published as *What the Kite Thinks* by Summer Session, University of Hawaiʻi at Mānoa in 1994.